THE WHOLE ARMOUR OF GOD
BY

John Henry Jowett

FOREWORD

John Henry Jowett (1863-1923) was a British Protestant teacher and writer whose books centered around Christian living.

The Whole Armour of God

I: THE INVISIBLE ANTAGONISMS

Eternal God, may no distraction draw us away from our communion with Thee. May we come to Thee like children going home, jubilant and glad. We have been in the far country and our garments are stained. May we hasten to the ministry of forgiveness and reconciliation. If we have been on fields of heavy battle, where the fire of the enemy has been awful and unceasing, may we hasten to Thee for the overhauling of our armor, and for the renewal of our strength. If we have been called upon to walk weary roads of unfamiliar sorrow, may we turn to Thee as to refreshing springs. If we have lapsed from our high calling, may we renew our covenant. If we have missed a gracious opportunity, may we seek another chance. If we have been counted faithful in any service, and have fulfilled our commission by the help of Thy grace, may we hasten to give the glory to Thee. Unite us, we humbly pray Thee, in the holy bonds of Christian sympathy. Deepen our pity so that we may share the sorrows of people far away. May we feel the burden of the burdened and weep with them that weep. May we not add to our sin by ceasing to remember those who are in need. Grant peace in our time, O Lord, the peace which is the fruit of righteousness. Let Thy will be done among all the peoples, so that in common obedience to Thee all the nations may find abiding union. Amen.

"Wherefore take unto you the whole armour of God, that ye may be able to withstand in the evil day, and having done all to stand." Eph. 6:13.

Let me give one or two other translations which devout scholars have made in the attempt to bring out the precise significance of Paul's original words. Many interpreting minds act like the solar spectrum, and they help to display the wealthy contents in the pure white light of gospel truth. Here then is Dr. Moffatt's translation: "So take God's armour that you may be able to make a stand in the evil day and hold your ground by overcoming all your foes." And here is Dr. Weymouth's fine attempt to elicit the buried wealth of the apostle's words: "Put on the complete armour of God so that you may be able to stand your ground on the day of battle, and having fought to the end to remain victors on the field." That is a translation which stirs one's blood, and I am inclined to regard it as a very vital interpretation of the rousing, soldierly counsel of the apostle Paul.

The apostle is writing to a tiny company of Christians at Ephesus, so tiny that they are like a drop in a bucket in the midst of that teaming population. For this is what has happened. Under the constraining influence of the gospel of Christ this little handful of men and women have done one of the hardest things we are ever called upon to do. They have cut themselves away from old fellowships. They have separated themselves from the fond attachments of a lifetime. They have severed themselves from venerable roots. They have forfeited dear and vital friendships, and they are now living an alien life within the circle of their own city. They are strangers in their own home. They are foreigners in their native land. They are pilgrims in their own country. They are in it and yet not of it. They are like tropical plants which find themselves in the Arctic Zone. And it is to this little company that the apostle writes this letter, and to them he gives the inspiring counsel of my text: "Put on the complete armour of God that ye may be able to stand your ground in the day of battle."

In what sort of circumstances did these people live? Let us take a swift survey of the hostility of their surroundings. What was the nature of the antagonisms by which this little company were beset? First of all, there was the overwhelming power of the world. Their city itself was luxuriously placed. The very location of Ephesus was favourable to prosperity, enjoying as it did the double advantage of shelter and of openness to the outer world. I was amazed when I walked among its ruins in the late spring at the magnificence of its position. If you will think of a cup, with more than a third of its rim broken down to its base, you will gain a rough but practical suggestion of the groundwork of this ancient city. About two-thirds of the city are immediately engirt with noble and richly verdured hills. Then this sheltering rim of hills is broken, and the cup opens out in one direction to a port on the open sea, and in the other direction to a rich alluvial plain, famous for its wonderful fertility. Such was Ephesus, sheltered and yet open, with protective arms of hills about it, and yet widely hospitable to the trade and wealth of the world. No wonder Ephesus was luxurious, no wonder she was carnal, and no wonder she was ennervated. She was the very hunting ground of the garish world, and in this mesmeric garishness this little company of Christians had their home. This was the first of their antagonisms.

Well, then, to mention a second antagonism, there was the majestic power of an alien religion. The magnificent Temple of Diana, which is now only a little heap of stones, with literally not one stone resting orderly upon another, then dominated the city by its splendour, and represented a religion which held the people in the loose leash of easy and licentious morals. Just think of that resplendent temple, that gorgeous temple, and then think of some obscure house in some obscure street, where this little company of Christians met to commune with their Lord, and in the contrast you will realize another of the antagonisms which assailed their discipleship every hour of the day. The Temple of Diana versus the little Christian meeting-house! It makes one think of another contrast in the grey and windy city of Edinburgh; the dark, frowning Palace of Holyrood versus John Knox's small house in Canongate! And history tells us which of these two proved to be the dwelling-place of invincible strength. This was the second of their antagonisms.

And then, to name a third of their antagonisms, there was the pervasive power of popular customs and traditions. Every day this little handful of Christians were up against customs that were like invisible bonds. Yes, religious and social customs always thread the common life, and to oppose them is to run up against antagonisms which are like invisible webs of barbed wire. We know what it means to oppose a popular custom to-day. Just oppose even a simple one; decide to wear no black in the hour of bereavement and you are up against a world of hostility and suspicion. And, still further, let the convention you defy be an ecclesiastical convention, or one which has somehow come to wear religious sanctions, and the antagonism is tremendous. Well, this little company of Christians in Ephesus were defying popular social customs and popular religious customs every day, and they were, therefore, confronted with a fierce and terrific opposition. And so they had all these antagonisms to meet, the hardening glare of the world, the far-reaching power of an alien religion, and the tyranny of popular custom and tradition. And in the very thick of all these you must imagine these comparatively youthful Christians seeking to live their separate and consecrated life.

But in this strong and tender letter to this little flock of Christians, the apostle Paul looks beyond the opposition of flesh and blood, and the steely barriers of usage and tradition; he pierces the visible veil and beholds invisible antagonists, spiritual, alive, active and hostile. Listen to him: "For ours is not a conflict with mere flesh and blood, but with the despotisms, the empires, the forces that control and govern this dark world, the spiritual hosts of evil arrayed against us in the heavenly warfare." When the apostle looked upon Ephesus it seemed as though the whole city became transparent, and behind the visible and transient veils he saw these spiritual foes. There was much mischief in Ephesus, there was much weaving of evil webs, there was much coming and going of worldly forces; but to Paul, the real prompters and instigators were back in the unseen. This is the teaching of this great apostle. These Christians in the early Church had to fight unseen enemies, antagonists in the spirit—"spiritual hosts of evil in the heavenly warfare." The real enemy is entrenched in the unseen, and he is ever active, night and day, and the early believer confronted him in ancient Ephesus, as the later believer confronts him in modern New York and London.

Now it is of these invisible antagonists that the apostle most urgently warns these young disciples. He warns them of the extraordinary subtlety of the warfare, of the wiles of the devil, of the stratagems of these mysterious powers, of their traps and devices, of their diabolic cleverness, and of their amazing and manifold ingenuities. The instruments of modern material warfare are almost incredible in the refinement of their destructiveness, and I have no doubt in my own mind that even these ingenuities are also diabolic, and that if we could pierce the veil we should see the invisible enemies at their fiendish work. But these unseen antagonists out-do all the subtleties of the material instruments of destruction in the devices in which they lure and snare and entrap and overthrow the soul.

Well, then, how do these antagonists work? How is this cunning antagonism exerted upon the soul? It is exerted both mediately and immediately. First of all, these invisible antagonists work immediately upon the soul. Spirit can work upon spirit; mind can lay pressure upon mind. There is a direct and immediate influence upon the secret life of man. That is the teaching of the Word of God, and I freely confess to you that there are phenomena in my own life, and in the lives of others which I cannot interpret in any other way. I know it is altogether mysterious, but it is by no means incredible. In our own day we are obtaining first glimpses into avenues of spiritual activity which hitherto have been shrouded in mist and darkness. The phenomena of thought transference, of telepathy, of hypnotism, are lifting the veil upon modes of influence of which we have scarcely dreamed. One mind can influence another mind directly without either speech or deed, leaving upon the other the seal and imprint of its own mould. When I see this I do not count it incredible when it is reported to me that there are spiritual antagonists in Ephesus and in New York who prey upon the thoughts of man, and work upon his imagination, and engage his sentiments and ambitions with the purpose of luring him from his sacred loyalties, and inciting him to rebellion against the holy and most high God. "Ours is not a conflict with mere flesh and blood," says the apostle. We have invisible foes.

And then, in the second place, these spiritual antagonists work mediately upon the soul. They work upon the soul through the medium of human ministries—through the contagious power of crowds, through the gravitation of the age, through the general spirit of society, through the psychological climate in which our life is cast. And they also work upon the soul through the medium of individuals, through men and women who have been captured by the evil one and who are now used in his purposes of moral and spiritual destruction. Our invisible antagonists cast their lure upon us through the ministry of our fellow-men.

Now all these antagonisms, seen and unseen, mediate and immediate, this little company of Christians had to meet in ancient Ephesus. You say the antagonisms are tremendous! Yes, indeed they are, and the Christian life is a tremendous thing. That is what tens of thousands of professing Christians have yet to learn. Let it be said that of all tremendous things the Christian life is the most tremendous. It is not something we can play with in idle hours, it is not a merely pleasant fellowship, it is not the bloodless act of joining the visible Church. No, it is not the carrying of a highly imposing label; it is a desperate, continuous, but withal, a glorious campaign. Speaking for myself, I confess that I have to have my fingers on the throat of the devil every day of my mortal life. This is how I find it. I do not gain a single inch without a fight. No fine victory is ever gained by me without blood. O, the sternness of the Christian fight! and O, its attractiveness and its glory! Yes, indeed, you are right; the antagonisms are tremendous.

How then, are they to be met? If these are our antagonisms, seen and unseen, in New York as well as in Ephesus, how can we meet and overcome them? Let us listen to the Word: "Put on the complete armour of God." Let us begin there. Our first need is God. Without God we are beaten even before the fight begins. We have no more likelihood of vanquishing our spiritual foes without God than this unaided hand of mine would be able to drive back the solid phalanxes of the German hosts. We must begin with God. In the tenth verse of this chapter the apostle unfolds the primary secret of victory. "Be strong in the Lord and in the power of His might." But that is a very imperfect translation, laying too much emphasis upon the soldier and too little upon his Lord. I greatly like the marginal rendering of the revised version: "Be made powerful in the Lord." Does not that word sound full of promise for soldiers who are about to storm a difficult position? "Be made powerful in the Lord." Let God make you powerful! Such power is not a trophy of battle; it is the fruit of communion. It is a bequest and not a conquest. This power is not something we have to win; it is something we have to receive. It is not something we have to gain; it is something we have to take. "Be made powerful in the Lord!" And listen again: "Ye shall receive power when the Holy Spirit is come upon you." That power, that vital endowment of strength, is the gift of God, one of the ministries of the divine grace, and it is offered to every soldier without money and without price. So is it true that our first necessity in battle is to hasten away to the Lord to receive the gifts of the soldier's strength.

But not only is there the imperative need of God for our initial strength, but for every piece of armour which may be needful in the fight. Armour for offence, and armour for defence; armour to meet every device and stratagem with which we may be assailed. I propose to consider this armour, piece by piece, and over and over again I shall have to tell you that you may find every piece of armour in the abundantly stocked and open and free armoury of God. And therefore do I say again that if we are to be triumphant over our antagonists, our first need is God. "Seek ye the Lord." "O come, let us kneel before the Lord our Maker."

And then, our other great requirement is the ceaseless co-operation of our wills. The life of a Christian soldier is not a continuous reclining on "flowery beds of ease." Having obtained the strength we must ceaselessly exercise it in the practice of our wills. Listen to the divine challenge to the will: "Be made powerful in the Lord!" Well, then, exercise the will you have, your weak will, and go and kneel in humility at the source of power, and receive the promised gift. "Put on the whole armour of God!" Well, then, exercise the will and go to the armoury of grace for thine arms. "Stand therefore!" Well, then, having received the gift of power, exercise thy will in stubborn and invincible resistance. "Here stand I," said one who had received the strength, "Here stand I; I can do no other, God help me!" "Having done all, stand"—and victory shall be yours! In the name of God the Father, God the Son, and God the Holy Spirit, victory shall most certainly be yours!

Says Dr. Weymouth: "Stand your ground in the day of battle, and having fought to the end remain victors on the field." "Victors on the field." I am thrilled by the inspiring word—"Victors on the field." After every temptation—the temptation that comes to me in sunshine, or the temptation that comes to me in the gloom—after every fight, victors on the field! The Lord's banner flying, His banner of love and grace; and the evil one and all his host in utter rout, and in full and dire retreat!

Soldiers of Christ arise,
And put your armour on;
Strong in the strength which God supplies
Through His eternal Son.

II: THE GIRDLE OF TRUTH

Holy Father, we humbly pray Thee to reveal unto us the unsearchable riches of Christ. Refine our discernments in order that we may behold them; and deepen our hearts in order that we may long to possess them. Unveil to us our poverty so that we may seek Thy wealth. Lead us through meekness and penitence to the reception of spiritual power. May our loins be girt about with truth. May we drink deeply at the waters of promise and find refreshment in immediate duty. We pray that Thou wilt bind us together in the bonds of holy sympathy. Help us to gather up the needs of others in common intercession. Make us ready to bear the burden of the race. Quicken our imaginations in order that we may enter into the sorrows of Thy children in every land. We humbly pray Thee to steady our faith in these days of bewilderment. In all the confusion of our time may we never lose sight of Thy throne. In all the obscuring of our ideals may we never lose sight of Christ. And O, Lord, out of our disorder may we be led into larger ways. Let Thy Holy Spirit brood over us, quickening all that is full of sacred promise, and destroying all that hinders our friendship with Thee. Amen.

"Stand therefore, having your loins girt about with truth." Eph. 6:14.

The girdle was just a strong belt holding the different pieces of a soldier's armour securely in their place. Even in the ordinary Oriental attire the girdle was a necessity. Without the girdle the loose, flowing garments became very cumbersome, flapping about the feet, and especially hindering the movements in a hostile wind. Even the most graceful attire became an entanglement unless the girdle held it in serviceable bonds. But the necessity of a girdle was still more imperative on the field of war. In active fighting loose pieces of armour would be like embarrassing articles hanging on the soldier rather than appropriate implements to make him efficient. Loose armour was troublesome and distressing, making the soldier feel soft, and awkward, and unready, giving him a sense of going to pieces. The belt bound the loose pieces together, creating a healthy sense of firmness, compactness, and making the soldier feel that he had everything well in hand, and enabling him to meet the enemy's attack with united strength and confidence.

Now it is that figure of the military belt which the apostle is using in our text, "Let your loins be girt about with truth." The soldier of Jesus can have his armour flapping about him in disorderly array. He can be loose and distracted. His energies can be scattered. He can be just a mass of incoherences and inconsistencies in the presence of the foe. Or a soldier of Jesus can be firm, and collected, and decisive. He can be "all there," with every ounce of his strength available for the immediate fight. And the apostle teaches that this bracing sense of collectedness, this fine, firm feeling of moral and spiritual concentration, can only be obtained by binding the entire life with the splendid and tenacious girdle of gospel truth.

I want to approach the apostle's central teaching along roads which will gather up the testimony of common experience. We all know the strength which is imparted to a life when it is girt about with firm principle. It is even so in the life of a boy when he is passing his earliest days at school. Is there anything nobler to contemplate than a fine boy whose life and character are held firm and free in the bond and girdle of moral principle? It is even so in the later days of college and university. What college or university graduate has not admired the decisive strength of some man or woman whose character was held in splendid consistency by the girdle of moral conviction! What joyful and boisterous liberty there is in such a life! And it is all the more free and jubilant because it recognizes fields of license into which it never strays. And in the broader fields of the world we have the witness of the same experience. Life that is held in a girdle quadruples its strength. Life which is bound together even by a strong expediency gathers force in the bondage. A life which is held in the constraint of a policy is far mightier than a life which is trailing in scattered indifference. But a life which is bound together in moral principle, having all its faculties and powers gathered under one control, has tremendous force both of attack and resistance.

You may study the contents of that statement and find abundant illustrations in the lives of men like Lincoln, and Mazzini, and Gladstone, and John Bright, and John Morley, and James Bryce. All these men, whether we approve or disapprove their political programmes and ambitions, are men whose characters reveal no loose ends, no trailing garments, no unchartered opinions, no vagrant and unlicensed moods, but rather a moral wholeness and solidity which we know will retain its splendid consistency in the teeth of the fiercest storm. Yes, even in the ways of the world men recognize the man who is wearing the belt of principle, and whose loins are girt about with truth.

But the apostle Paul is thinking of something more than moral principle, splendid as is the influence of a great principle on the healthy action of a life. He is thinking of something even finer and deeper than this, and in which the moral principle is included. He is thinking of a soul belted with the more distinctive truth of the Scriptures, a soul girt about with gospel truth and with the ample promises of God. He is thinking of a man who takes some great truth of revelation, some mighty word of life, or some broad and bracing promise of grace, and who belts it about his soul and wears it on active service in seeking to do the sovereign will. I know not where to begin, or where to end, when I turn to the pages of biography for examples of men and women who have worn the girdle of gospel truth and promise. Let me dip here and there in the many and brilliant records.

Well, then, let us begin with Martin Luther. It is one of the strong characteristics of Luther that he is ever wearing the girdle of truth, and bracing himself with the promises of grace. I open his letters almost at random, in the great year of his life when he defied the pope, and opposed himself to the strength of uncounted hosts. He is writing to Melanchthon on May 26, 1521: "Do not be troubled in spirit; but sing the Lord's song in the night, as we are commanded, and I shall join in. Let us only be concerned about the Word." There you find him putting on the girdle! Once again I find him writing a letter to a poor little company of Christians at Wittenberg: "I send you this thirty-seventh Psalm for your consolation and instruction. Take comfort and remain steadfast. Do not be alarmed through the raging of the godless." There again he is wearing the girdle and urging others to wear it. His loins are girt about with truth.

Then again there is John Wesley. Let me give you a glimpse of that noble servant of the spirit as he is putting on the girdle of truth: "When I opened the New Testament at five o'clock in the morning my eyes fell on the words, 'There are given unto us exceeding great and precious promises that we should be partakers of the divine nature.'" He girt his loins with that truth. "Just before I left the room I opened the Book again, and this sentence gleamed from the open page, 'Thou art not far from the Kingdom of God.'" And he girt himself with that promise. He went to St. Paul's that morning, and in the chant there came to him this personal message from the Word: "O Israel, trust in the Lord, for in the Lord there is mercy and in Him there is plenteous redemption, and He shall redeem Israel from all his sins." Do you not see this noble knight belting himself for the great crusade that even now awaits him at the gate?

Then I think I will mention General Gordon, who laid down his life at Khartoum. Only, if you want to see Gordon girding himself with truth, and see it adequately, you will have to quote from almost every letter he ever wrote, and especially his wonderful correspondence with his sister. Take this sentence from a letter written in Cairo in 1884: "I have taken the words, 'He will hide me in His hands'; good-night, my dear sister, I am not moved, even a little." Or take this sentence from a letter written in Khartoum toward the end of his days: "This word has been given me, 'It is nothing to our God to help with many or with few,' and I now take my worries more quietly than before." He put on the girdle of truth, and his worries were leashed in the girdle, and his soul was quieted in gospel confidence and serenity.

And I had other examples to offer you, but these must suffice. I had on my table David Livingstone, and John Woolman, and Josephine Butler, and Frances Willard, and Catherine Booth, and I wanted to give you glimpses of all these notable soldiers of the Lord girding themselves for the open field. But their names shall be their witness. I might have quoted, had I the knowledge and the time, the testimony of all the saints who from their labours rest. And concerning them all we should have seen that their loins were girt about with truth.

Now it was to spiritual equipment of this kind that the apostle was directing the little company of Christians at Ephesus. Think of their surroundings:—the overwhelming worldliness, the dominating influence of an alien religion, the fierce antagonisms of popular customs and traditions, and all of these backed by invisible hosts of wickedness in heavenly places. Now what chance would a loose, shuffling Christian have in circumstances so hostile as these? The Christian in Ephesus, if he is to be a conqueror, must not slouch along the way with a loose, hang-dog sort of air, but rather with all the poise and movement of a lion. The Christian must belt himself about with big truth, truth that will not only confirm but invigorate, truth that will not only define his creed but vitalize his soul. And these Ephesian Christians followed the apostle's counsel and they girded themselves with truth, and so were able to stand in the evil day, and having done all, to stand.

Let us watch how they did it. They had been converted to the Christian faith and life. One sure effect of their conversion was a more vivid sense of sin. After their conversion their own sinfulness began to reveal itself in more awful relief. The nearer they got to the light the more their sin appeared, just like invisible writing emerging from its secrecy when exposed to the open fire. They saw their sin, and they saw the sin of the people. They were like the prophet Isaiah, to whom also there came the awakening sense of sin, and with him they could have cried: "Woe is me, for I am unclean, and I dwell in the midst of a people of unclean lips." Well, now, how could that little company of Christians deal with the sin? It was like trying to drain a vast and bitter marsh that was fed by secret springs. How could they do it? And the tremendous task only emphasized their weakness, and might have depressed them into a feeling of helplessness and despair. And we share that feeling to-day. Think of the colossal sins of Europe, and think of the sins and moral indifference of the great cities. If the sin be like a bitter marsh, what is going to drain it? Nay, how are we going to get the confidence that it can be drained? Well what did Paul do, and what did he teach his fellow-disciples to do? This is what he did. He found something even bigger than sin, and he girded himself with the bigger thing when he confronted the appalling task. Listen to him: "Where sin abounds grace does much more abound." Yes, sin is a big thing, but grace is a bigger thing; the biggest thing even in this rebellious and indifferent world. Sin is a strong thing, but grace is a stronger thing, even the strongest thing in a revolting and alienated world. Well then, let your loins be girt about with that truth! Put it around your fears and uncertainties like a strong girdle. Wear it ever night and day. Go up to every stupendous task in the vigour of its bracing grip. Begin at the piece of the bitter marsh nearest to you, and begin to drain it. And wear the truth—"Where sin abounds, grace doth much more abound." Wear the truth, say it, sing it, and you will be amazed how the difficulty will be subdued; for the mouth of the Lord hath spoken it.

There was something else in Ephesus for which these Christians needed the girdle of truth. Ephesus was a vast city, and these Christians were only a tiny and obscure fellowship. And even this small fellowship had to be broken up during the hours of labour, and in those hours each believer had to stand alone. One of them was perhaps a slave, and there was no fellow-believer in the house. Or perhaps one was a soldier, and there wasn't another believer in his regiment, and he had to face it all alone. We have been reading that one reason for the massed solidity of the German advance is that the individual German soldier craves the mystic strength of fellowship, and desires even the physical touch of a comrade-in-arms. I can understand it. And so could the Ephesian Christians have understood it. They felt strong when they touched their fellow-believers, and they felt weakened when the visible communion was broken.

What, then, shall they do when alone? They must let their loins be girt about with truth. But what truth? What did the apostle Paul wear in such isolation? He took this girdle and wrapped it round his loins: "He loved me, and gave Himself for me." And that girdle gives a man a sense of glorious fellowship along the emptiest and loneliest road. Put that girdle on, lonely soul! "He loves me, and gave Himself for me!" Wear it ever, night and day. And wear it consciously! Say it; sing it—"He loved me, and gave Himself for me." "Let your loins be girt about with that truth."

And so have we seen these Ephesian soldiers putting on the girdle. In the presence of threat and persecution they wore this girdle, "We are more than conquerors through Him that loved us." When their circumstances were a medley and a confusion, full of ups and downs, of strange comings and goings, of mingled joy and sorrow, foul and fair, they wore this girdle: "All things work together for good to them that love God." And thus they were braced for all the changes of the ever-changing day.

So do I urge my fellow-soldiers in this later day to wear the belt. "Let your loins be girt about with truth." Let us pray the good Lord to help us even now to put it on. Is the girdle we need this—"He loved me and gave Himself for me?" Well, put it on. Or is it this—"We have forgiveness through His blood?" Put it on. Or is it this—"I will come again and receive you unto myself?" Put it on. Or is it this—"In My Father's house are many mansions?" Put it on. Or is it this—"I will never leave thee nor forsake thee?" Put it on. Or is it this great girdle—"When thou passest through the waters I will be with thee, and through the rivers, they shall not overthrow thee, when thou walkest through the fire thou shalt not be burned, neither shall the flame kindle upon thee?" Put on the girdle, wear it ever, night and day, and thou shalt find that in the strength of gospel truth thou are competent to meet all circumstances, and triumphantly perfect thy Saviour's will.

III: THE BREASTPLATE OF RIGHTEOUSNESS

Almighty God, our Father, it is by Thy grace that we attain unto holiness, and it is by Thy light that we find wisdom. We humbly pray that Thy grace and light may be given unto us so that we may come into the liberty of purity and truth. Wilt Thou graciously exalt our spirits and enable us to live in heavenly places in Christ Jesus. Impart unto us a deep dissatisfaction with everything that is low, and mean, and unclean, and create within us such pure desire that we may appreciate the things which Thou hast prepared for them that love Thee. Wilt Thou receive us as guests of Thy table. Give us the glorious sense of Thy presence, and the precious privilege of intimate communion. Feed us with the bread of life; nourish all our spiritual powers; help us to find our delight in such things as please Thee. Give us strength to fight the good fight of faith. Give us holy courage, that we may not be daunted by any fear, or turn aside from our appointed task. Make us calm when we have to tread an unfamiliar road, and may Thy presence give us companionship divine. Amen.

"Having on the breastplate of righteousness." Ephesians 6:14.

This is counsel given to a little company of Christians, so little as to be almost submerged and lost in the great unfriendly city of Ephesus, so little as to be like a tiny boat in the midst of a vast and threatening sea. A missionary of the gospel has been among them and they have received the word of the Lord Jesus. They have answered the constraint of redeeming love and they have confessed their faith in Christ. And what has happened? Their confession has compelled their separation from many of their old fellowships and attachments. They are loosened from many of their old affections. The forces that were once friendly to them have become unfriendly, and they are now confronted by overwhelming hostilities on every side.

We must try to feel the power and peril of their isolation if we would understand the force of the apostle's words. Imagine then the lot of some German in Germany who espoused the cause of the Allies, or conceive the lot of some Englishman in England who sided with Germany, and you may realize the heat and fierceness of the antagonism with which these immature Christians were surrounded in the city of Ephesus. But their peril was not only found in the hostility of their old friends. There was the enervating moral atmosphere which they had to breathe; there was the recurring inclination of their own riotous passions; there was a remnant of appetite for the old delights; and there was the nervous fear that the forces against them might prove overwhelming.

What should they do? How should they be able to stand? And especially how should they be able to stand in the evil day, the day when external circumstances might culminate in some terrific assault, or when their own passions might rise against them in some particularly fierce resurgence? Well, this chapter records the counsel of a great and experienced apostle, a mighty soldier of the Lord, in which he advises these young recruits of the Kingdom what armour they must wear if they would be victorious on the field. "Put on the whole armour of God." And we are considering these noble pieces of armour if haply we too may possess the equipment and so turn our days of battle into days of glorious victory.

And now, in the name of the Lord Jesus, I bring you this piece of armour, "the breastplate of righteousness," and it is to be worn in our modern warfare in this difficult city of New York. What is this breastplate of righteousness? What indeed was the Roman breastplate from which the figure of speech is taken? Unfortunately, the word breastplate is very inaccurate and misleading. The piece of armour to which the apostle refers protected the back as well as the breast, and in addition it gave protection to the neck and the hips. It would be much more truly described by the phrase, "a coat of mail," because it was a sort of vest made of small metal plates, overlapping one another like shield upon shield, wrapping the body in its defences, and protecting the vital organs, back and front, from every assault of the foe.

Let us then venture to lift this more accurate description into our text, "Put on righteousness like a coat of mail, wear it in all your comings and goings in the city of Ephesus, and in it meet all the malicious antagonisms of devils and of men." Now I wonder how the apostle's counsel affected these fearful struggling Christians in Ephesus. Let us look at them. Let us assume that we are with them, and that we are about to give them the counsel offered in the text. How will they receive it? Remember that they have just been lifted out of the horrible pit and out of the miry clay of long-continued sin, and that they are oppressed by their own weakness and helplessness, and by the strength of the evil inclinations and habits which they have just renounced. Well, now, let us offer these inexperienced disciples the apostle's counsel: "Put on righteousness like a coat of mail!" Why, they just look at you in utter despair! It is their very weakness that they cannot forge and weave such a coat of mail to cover them in the day of battle. The counsel would surely seem like the taunting cry of the foe.

Suppose we had waylaid poor Christian in "The Pilgrim's Progress" when he was struggling with his oppressive burden up the hill, and with the fiery darts of the devil hurtling around him on every side, and suppose we had called out to him, "Put on righteousness like a coat of mail!" We should surely only have added heaviness to his burden and crushed him to the ground in despair. "Put on righteousness like a coat of mail?" he would have moaned in his reply, "My righteousness is like unto filthy rags!"

One poor, sorrowful correspondent wrote to me some weeks ago who was the victim of alcohol and drugs. For years he had walked in ways of uncleanness, but he was now just waking from his awful sleep and turning his thoughts toward home. Suppose now I had written to him and said "Put on righteousness like a coat of mail!" I think his eyes would have dulled into weariness again, and he would have slipped back to his drugs and his despair. This cannot be the meaning of the apostle's counsel, or this coat of mail would never be worn.

What, then, does the apostle mean when he says "Put on righteousness like a coat of mail"? Let us seek for light in his own life, for he is a soldier as well as a counsellor, and we shall find him following his own advice and wearing the armour which he recommends to others. Let us listen then to this word, and let us mark its significance; "Touching the righteousness which is in the law I was found blameless." That seems like an invincible protection. "Touching the righteousness which is in the law I was found blameless!" But there was nothing invincible about it. It was no more a coat of mail than an ordinary vest, and the devil smote through the defences a dozen times a day.

Listen again to the apostle when he has passed into the intimate friendship of Christ: "Not having a righteousness of mine own." Mark that; yea verily mark that;—"Not having a righteousness of mine own." This coat of mail he wears is not his own righteousness. Whose, then, is it? It is the righteousness of Christ. As Paul declares: "It is the righteousness which is through the faith of Christ, the righteousness which is of God by faith." The apostle is wearing the righteousness of Christ, and he wears it like a coat of mail, covering back and front, shielding him before and behind.

I want to pause a little there because we are very near one of the deepest mysteries in the gospel of grace, and I want to state the mystery as plainly as words can express it. This, then, is what the Scriptures state: The Lord Jesus Christ was absolutely righteous, so righteous that human imagination and human dream cannot conceive it excelled. His holy obedience was perfect. There was no rent in the vesture of His holiness. There was no frayed edge, there was no imperfect strand, there were no stains. "In Him was no sin." We must begin there.

And now let us assume that a poor penitent comes to this perfectly holy Lord. Let us make the sinner as nauseous and repulsive as you please. Let us make him a moral leper, the wretched victim of uncleanness, befouled by his own habits, consumed in his own sin, eaten without and within. That poor penitent sinner, laden with defilement, comes to the holy Lord Jesus, humbly seeking His favour and grace.

Now what happens? What do the Scriptures tell us about the happening? They tell us that the holy Saviour covers the sinner with the robe of His own righteousness. The Lord puts His merits on to the sinner who has no merits. He puts His obedience on to the sinner who has nothing but a record of disobedience. He puts His spiritual conquests on to the sinner who is torn and scarred by nothing but appalling defeats. He puts His holiness on to a sinner who has been raked by defilements. That is the proclamation of the gospel. That poor penitent believing sinner stands now before the devil, and before men and angels, and before the presence of God, clothed in the righteousness of Christ! What, in all his imperfections? Yes. In all his weaknesses? Yes. With the scorching marks of hell-fire still upon him? Yes. He is covered with the robe of Christ's righteousness. He wears the merits and the strength and the defences of the Lord's obedience. Have we not read of one who wrapped himself in his country's flag and then dared an alien power to fire? It is an altogether imperfect illustration, but it offers me some faint and helpful analogy when I hear the saints give this witness: "He hath clothed me with the robe of righteousness, and covered me with the garments of salvation." No, it was not Paul's own righteousness which constituted his coat of mail. It was the righteousness of his Lord.

Now, this is the word of grace, and this is the message of the gospel. It is this of which Toplady sings in his immortal hymn—"Rock of Ages":

"Naked, look to Thee for dress."

It is this also of which Charles Wesley sings in his also immortal hymn—"Jesus, Lover of my Soul":

"I am all unrighteousness,
Thou art full of truth and grace."

It is this which was discovered by George Fox, the founder of the Society of Friends, and of which he tells us so rapturously in the early pages of his journal. It was this which John Bunyan found, and of which he tells us in the pages of "Grace Abounding": "One day, as I was passing into the field, and that too with some dashes on my conscience, suddenly this sentence fell upon my soul, 'Thy righteousness is in heaven,' and me thought that I saw with the eyes of my soul, Jesus Christ at God's right hand. There, I saw, was my righteousness; so that wherever I was, or whatever I was doing, God could not say of me, He wants my righteousness, for that was just before Him. I also saw, moreover, that it was not my good frame of heart that made my righteousness better, nor yet my bad frame that made my righteousness worse; for my righteousness was Jesus Christ Himself, the same yesterday, to-day and forever. Now did my chains fall off my legs indeed; I was loosened from my afflictions and irons.... Now went I also home rejoicing for the grace and love of God." All these men, at the beginning of their Christian life, were covered not with a righteousness of their own, but with the righteousness of Christ, and they could sing with Paul that they were clothed in the garments of His salvation. Their coat of mail was the righteousness of Christ.

Now I recognize, and I experience the difficulty, of realizing all this, and I sympathize with you in the poverty of our apprehension. But I think our difficulty is in some ways occasioned by the inadequacy of all figures of speech to convey to us the real vitality of the truth. For instance, a coat of mail is something detached, separate and external, and so is a robe, and they have no vital relation to the body which wears them. And therefore, when we think of the righteousness of Christ covering another like a robe or a coat of mail, it appears something unreal, a superficial ministry, or even a fine pretence. We think of some villain clothed in the garb of a minister, but all the more a villain because of the robes which cover him. Or we think of some vile woman wearing the habits of a nun, and all the more vile because of the significant garments in which she is clothed. A leprous sinner wearing the robe of Christ's righteousness! It all appears detached and superficial, like a climbing rose hiding a rubbish heap, or some lovely ferns and greenery concealing an open sewer. There appears no deep reality in it,—a sinner just covered with the robe of Christ's holiness, and wearing the Lord's righteousness as a coat of mail.

Yes, I admit that the figures all fail. The figure of a robe leaves the sinner and the Saviour in no vital relation. And so it is with the coat of mail. But in the blessed reality there is no detachment. There is union between the sinner and the Saviour of the most profound and vital kind. You must remember our assumption; the sinner who comes to the Saviour comes in faith, and in penitence and in prayer, and these things never leave a soul separate and detached from the life and love of the Lord. Faith itself, even amid human relationships, is never a dividing ministry; it always consolidates and unites. You may trace the vital unifying influence of faith in a score of relations. The faith which a patient has in a doctor is a minister of very vital union in every effort to recover the lost genius of health. The faith which a pupil has in a teacher unites the two in a very vital relation, and puts the pupil into communion with the knowledge which is stored up in the teacher's mind. The faith which one man has in another incorporates the two in one. Faith always unifies; it never divides.

And all this has its supreme application in the relation of the soul to Christ. A poor penitent sinner who comes to the Lord in faith becomes one with the Lord in the profoundest union which the mind of man can conceive. Faith in Christ unites the soul with Christ just as in grafting the engrafted scion becomes one with the vital stock.

Now this is the beginning of our reasoning. We are assuming a poor, penitent, weary soul flinging himself by faith on Christ, and thereby becoming one with Christ, one with all He is; one with all He has been; one with all He shall be, sharing His merits, His holiness, His obedience! By faith in Christ I become one with Christ, and all He is is thrown over me! And now before the devil I stand as one in Christ; and in the day of judgment I shall stand as one in Christ, one with Him in spite of all the sins of my past, and all the weaknesses and immaturities of the present. "Thou hast covered me with the robe of righteousness, and clothed me in the garment of salvation." I wear the righteousness of Christ, and I wear it as a coat of mail.

Now is not that a strong defence? Go back to the illustration of grafting. I saw a young graft which had just been newly related to a strong and healthy stock. The graft still looked very poor and weak and sickly, but it had become vitally one with the healthy stock; it stood no longer in its own strength. All the resources of the stock were thrown about it, the merits of the stock were now the scion's, all the victories of its yesterdays, and all the sap and energies of to-morrow. The stock is to the scion as a coat of mail! And so it is with the soul which has become by faith the scion of the Lord.

"All my trust on Thee is stayed,
All my help from Thee I bring;
Cover my defenseless head
With the shadow of Thy wing."

The righteousness of Christ is the breastplate of the soul.

Now let us gather up our practical conclusions: The righteousness of Christ becomes immediately mine by the act and attitude of faith. Yea, verily, the most leprous and unclean soul in this city, with a history unutterably loathsome, whose faith looks up tremblingly to the Saviour, is immediately covered with the robe of Christ's righteousness, for by faith he immediately becomes one with the righteousness of Christ. By faith I can here and now become one with Christ; however poor and wretched I be, and however sinful I have been, the righteousness of Christ becomes the armour of my soul. You say that is very dogmatic. Yes, blessed be God, it is dogmatic, but it is justified dogmatism, for it is the glorious dogmatism of the gospel of Christ.

And covered with the righteousness of Christ, that imputed righteousness becomes progressively mine in the appropriation of experience. His life flows into me like the life of stock into scion, and all through my days I am assimilating more and more the righteousness which covers me. His covering righteousness becomes more and more my rectitude. His covering holiness becomes more and more my obedience. His righteousness passes more and more into my conscience and makes it holy; more and more into my affections and makes them lovely; more and more into my will to make it rich and dutiful in obedience. Forever and ever His righteousness will cover me, and forever and forever I shall be growing into His likeness. His righteousness is my defence. Yes, it is a coat of mail, a protection for breast and back. His righteousness protects me from the things that are behind, the guilt and the sins of my yesterdays. His righteousness protects me from the things of to-morrow, from all the assaults of the unknown way, from the fear of death, and from the day of judgment.

"When I soar through worlds unknown,
See Thee on Thy Judgment Throne,
Rock of Ages, cleft for me,
Let me hide myself in Thee."

IV: READY!

Heavenly Father, we thank Thee we are called to be children of the light. Even though we have been children of the darkness, and have loved the ways of error rather than of truth, and of sin rather than of holiness, Thou art calling us to the light of eternal day. We would answer Thy call in penitence, and we would return to Thee like wayward children who are coming home again. We do not ask to lose the sense of our shame, but we ask to taste the sweetness of Thy forgiveness. We do not ask to forget our rebelliousness, but we ask to be assured that we are reconciled to Thee. We would sit at Thy table and receive the bread of life. We would worship at Thy feet and receive the baptism of the Holy Spirit. We would stand before Thee with our feet shod with the shoes of readiness, willing to go out on errands of Christian love and service. If we are inclined to frivolity may we become inclined to be serious and reverent. If we are heedless may we become fired with heavenly ambition and spiritual devotion. Redeem us from the littleness of selfishness and lift us into the blessed communion of our fellow-men. Give us a wide and generous outlook upon human affairs. Endow us with the sympathy that rejoices with them who are rejoicing and that weeps with them that weep. If Thou art leading us through the gloom of adversity may we find that even the clouds drop fatness. If Thou art leading us through the green pastures and by the still waters, may we recognize the presence of the great Shepherd and may our joys be sanctified. Hallow all our experiences, we humbly pray Thee, and may we all become branches in the vine of our Lord. Amen.

"Your feet shod with the preparation of the gospel of peace." Ephesians 6:15.

A little while ago an article appeared in one of the daily papers with this startling title: "Boots and shoes may be vital determining factors in the war." And contrasts and comparisons were made between the opposing forces in respect to their footgear, and the provision which had been made for keeping the soldiers' feet strong and hardy. And allowing even for the ordinary journalistic exaggeration, it is a most reasonable thing to assume that good, durable, well-fitting boots are part of the requisite armour for all soldiers who are called to prolonged and exacting service. Think of those heavy tramps in the early days of the war, whether in advance or in retreat; and think of the miry roads and the marshy ground since the rains have fallen; and think of the wet and soaking trenches where the men have to stand for hours together; and you will begin to realize what a vital part boots may play in the terrible hardships of a long and wintry campaign.

In the Roman Empire scrupulous care was given to the feet of the fighting men. The shoes were specially made, not only for long marches, but for protection against the secret dangers of the way. They had not arrived at some of our refinements in devilry, but some of their subtleties occasioned great destruction. Gall-traps were set along the road, multitudes of sharp sticks were inserted on the surface of the road, keen as dagger points, to obstruct the advance of an enemy, and to maim his soldiers and compel them to fall out by the way. And so it was an imperative necessity that the Roman soldier be well shod, his feet made easy for the most exacting march, and defended against the hidden perils which would maim him in service and spoil him for the fray.

Now the apostle Paul had seen the Roman soldier marching as to war. I think he must have been particularly fond of watching soldiers because we can so often see and hear them reflected in his letters. We can always learn a great deal from a man by studying his metaphors and figures of speech, and we can get some very suggestive glimpses of his tastes and interests by watching the analogies of the apostle Paul, where the army is often tramping through his letters, and the Roman soldier is often presented to offer counsel to the soldiers of the Lord. And here in my text we are bidden to look to the soldier's shoes. He is well shod, so splendidly shod that in a moment he is ready for any call, along any road, and for any service.

And the Christian, too, has long marches, and often along difficult and trying roads, and there are flints about and sharp thorns, and other things that wound and make him stumble. And sometimes there is scarcely a road at all, and we have never been that way before, and it is like the work of a pioneer cutting his way through the jungle. What roads we have to tramp! Especially when we are apostles sent forth on the King's bidding! And, says the great apostle, "You need shoes for the roads or you will be unfit for the long journeys, and you will easily become tired and sore, and you may even drop out of the ranks." And what kind of shoes are we to wear as soldiers of Christ? How can we be defended in our long journeyings and in our crusades in the service of the King? The answer to these questions is given in the words: "Have your feet shod with the preparation of the gospel of peace." Now what is that?

Let me slightly recast the phrase. One of the words has slightly altered its colour and significance since the days of the Authorized Version. I mean the word "preparation." In the earlier days if you spoke of a man of "preparation" you meant a man who was prepared, a man who was equal to opportunity, a man who was awaiting the opening of the door, having everything ready for the call of obligation and service. So that the word "preparedness" would now be more accurate than the authorized word "preparation." "Having your feet shod with the preparedness of the gospel of peace." But I think we shall do even better if instead of either of these we use the word "readiness." "Having your feet shod with the readiness of the gospel of peace." What is that? Look at it a little more closely. "The readiness of the gospel"; that is the readiness which is born of the gospel as heat is born of the sun. The gospel of peace enters the soul of a man and takes possession of it, and then inspires the man with readiness. What for? Readiness to take the road to tell others the good tidings which have filled his own soul. That is it. The gospel of peace enters and glorifies the soul, and it then imparts to the feet a readiness to take the road, the long and difficult road, if need be, in order to tell to others the good news which has set it free. That is it. Have your feet shod with the readiness begotten of the gospel of peace!

Let me give an example, and let it be taken from the book of the prophet Isaiah. Here, then, are people in exile, sitting in the cold shadow of oppression, and longing for freedom and home. And over the hard mountain tracks there come messengers, swift messengers carrying the glad tidings of emancipation. There they come over the long roads! And when the suffering exiles see and hear them they break into this song: "How beautiful upon the mountains are the feet of him that bringeth good tidings, that publisheth peace; that bringeth good tidings of God, that publisheth salvation; that saith to Zion, Thy God reigneth! Break forth into joy! Sing together!" The feet of the messengers were shod with the readiness begotten of good news, and they were speeding with comfort to the desolate and distressed.

We have another example in the same book where messengers who were ladened with a rich experience were bidden to take the high road and tell their news to others. "O Zion, that bringest good tidings, get thee up into the high mountain; O Jerusalem, that bringest good tidings, lift up thy voice with strength; lift it up, be not afraid; say unto the cities of Judah, Behold your God!... He shall feed His flock like a shepherd: He shall gather the lambs with His arm, and carry them in His bosom; and shall gently lead those that are with young." That was the good news, and with the readiness begotten of the good news the messengers hastened to make it known. And so it is that our feet, as disciples of the Lord Jesus, are to be shod with similar readiness, the readiness begotten of our own experience of the goodness of God, the readiness to go out on the rough and troubled roads of life, into its highways and its byways, its broad streets and its narrow streets, carrying the good cheer of the news of God's redeeming love and grace. To be ready to go wherever there is any form of bondage, singing the gospel song of joy and freedom,—that is the privileged service of the soldiers of the Lord. "How beautiful upon the mountains are the feet of him that bringeth good tidings!" "Have your feet shod with the readiness of the gospel of peace."

Now I think it might be good for us to just glance along the roads of life and look at one or two sorts of people who are held in spiritual bondage, and who are therefore in need of good news and cheer, and we will challenge ourselves if our feet are shod with readiness to take them the gospel of peace. Well, then, look down this road, for here is a soul who is held in the bondage of despondency and despair. You will find such souls upon almost any road you like to tread. They are souls who somehow have fainted; they have lost the warm, cheering, kindling light of hope. Now failure is never really deadly until it puts out our hope and freezes the springs of resolution. The only really fatal element in defeat is the resolution not to try again. We have only terribly failed when we have furled our sails. Yes, I repeat it; failure only becomes virulent when it breeds despair.

Now these folk are on the road. They have so utterly failed that they have lost their vital confidence, and they have become pathetic victims of self-disparagement. What do they need? They need to have their lamps re-lit with the cheering light of hope. They need to have their fires rekindled with the blessed warmth of confidence. They need to hear of new dawnings, of radiant to-morrows, of larger, brighter coming days. And if they do need light and fire and sunrise, what is that but to say that they need to hear again the good tidings of the inexhaustible love of the risen Lord. They just need Jesus, and the comforting gospel of His peace.

Yes, but who is to take it? Messengers are wanted, messengers shod with "the readiness of the gospel of peace," messengers swift and ready to run these glorious errands as the ministers of eternal hope. Now, are we shod with that gospel readiness? Are our feet ready for the road? It is a noble and a gracious ministry. How beautiful upon the mountains are the feet of him that bringeth oil to smouldering lamps, and fuel to dying fires, and that cheer and illumine the cold haunts of despondency and despair! It is Mark Rutherford who says somewhere in what is to me an unforgettable word: "Blessed are they who heal us of our self-despisings." Yes, verily it is a beautiful ministry to kindle again the lovely light of confidence and hope. Are we ready for such service? Soldiers of Jesus, are our feet "shod with the readiness of the gospel of peace"?

Look again along the road. Here is another lonely soul, held in the bondage of a blinding experience. Let us say it is Saul of Tarsus, who is now on the road to Damascus: "And as he journeyed, he came near Damascus: and suddenly there shined round about him a light from heaven: and he fell to the earth, and heard a voice saying unto him: Saul, Saul, why persecuteth thou me?... And Saul arose from the earth, and when his eyes were opened he saw no man: but they led him by the hand and brought him into Damascus." Now here is a man who is held in the bondage of a blinding experience. He has been smitten in the midnight, but has not yet seen the dawn. He is convicted of sin, but has not yet found peace. He has lost his old life but has not yet found the new one. His old delights have gone, but the new joys have not yet arrived. He has been stunned, but he is not yet free! And there he is! What is needed? O surely, what is needed is some human messenger in whom the gospel of peace dwells like summer sunshine and fragrance, and whose feet are shod with readiness to carry that gracious summer to others. "And the Lord said unto Ananias, Arise and go into the street which is called Straight, and inquire in the house of Judas for one called Saul.... And Ananias went his way, and entered into the house; and putting his hands on him, said, Brother Saul, the Lord, even Jesus, that appeared unto thee on the way as thou camest, hath sent me, that thou mightest receive thy sight, and be filled with the Holy Ghost. And immediately there fell from his eyes as it had been scales." And so the blinded found his sight, and the enslaved found his liberty, and the bewildered found his peace; and one of the Lord's messengers was the human minister in the great emancipation. His feet were shod with the readiness of the gospel of peace. "How beautiful upon the mountains are the feet of him that bringeth good tidings."

There are other blinded people along the road, people who are stunned and bewildered, not by dazzling light but by fierce lightning. There are people who are just blinded by calamity. They have suffered the lightning stroke of disaster or bereavement. I was talking to one such troubled soul this very week; and speaking of the repeated blows of her heavy sorrows she said: "They just left me blind and dumb!" Blind and dumb along the road! What did she need? O, she just needed the restoring balm and cordials of heavenly comfort. She needed the soft consolations of divine grace. And what is that but to say again that she needed the gospel of peace? And where are the messengers, with feet shod with the readiness of the gospel of peace, to carry the good tidings to this soul held in the bondage of silence and night? How unspeakable is the privilege of carrying this holy grace, and seeing the holy light of faith breaking upon the face of bewilderment, lovelier far than the glory of sunrise breaking upon the mountains, flushing the cold snows, and suffusing with living color the gloominess of the pines! Yes, it is a beautiful service to carry good tidings to those who are stunned. "How beautiful upon the mountain are the feet of him that bringeth good tidings!" Soldiers of Jesus, are our feet shod with this readiness of the gospel of peace?

Look once more down the road, for there is another soul held in the bondage of ignorance. Let it be a man of Ethiopia. Let the road be the steep descent which leadeth down from Jerusalem to Gaza. "A man of Ethiopia, an eunuch of great authority under Candace, Queen of the Ethiopians, who had the charge of all her treasure, and did go to Jerusalem for to worship, was returning, and sitting in his chariot, read Esaias, the prophet." This man has the Word, but he has not got the clue. He has the Scriptures, but he has no interpreter. What is needed? He needs some messenger in whom the Word has become life, and who has discovered the central secret of the Scriptures in the companionship of the Lord. "The angel of the Lord spake unto Philip, saying, Arise, and go toward the south, unto the way that goeth down from Jerusalem unto Gaza. And he arose and went." "How beautiful upon the mountain are the feet of him that bringeth good tidings!" "And Philip ran thither to him, and heard him read the prophet Esaias." He ran on his errand because his feet were shod with readiness!

"Take my feet and let them be
Swift and beautiful for Thee."

"And Philip said, Understandest thou what thou readest?" So he explained to him the Word, and through the Word led him unto the Lord. And this is the last word we read about this man going down to Egypt: "He went on his way rejoicing!" What a ministry for a servant of the Lord! And that is your gracious service, fellow-preacher, in the ministry of the Word. And that is your privilege, Sunday-school teacher, when you meet your children in the class. You are appointed by the Lord to light up words that will burn in your scholars' minds to the very end of the pilgrim way. And that is the privilege of all of us if we will just have confidence in the guiding grace of the Lord. We need not be stars in order to light lamps and kindle fires. A taper is quite enough if it burns with genuine flame. Our greatest fitness for this kind of service is to be ready to do it, and the Lord Himself will provide the needful equipment. To have feet shod with readiness, that is what we need. Then through our ministry it may joyfully happen that many of

"The sons of ignorance and night
Will dwell in the eternal light
Through the eternal love."
There is only one thing remaining to be said. The apostle teaches that such readiness is armour for our own souls, it is defensive armour against the world, the flesh and the devil. To be ready to tell the good news of grace, the gospel of peace, is to have stout protection as you trudge along the road. Readiness is one piece of armour in the panoply of God. The soul which is not ready to serve is an easy prey to the evil one. A man whose feet are swift to carry the good tidings of grace is the favoured child of glorious promise: "He shall give His angels charge over thee, to keep thee in all thy ways." While we are ministering to others we are being ministered unto by the spirits that surround His throne, and our security is complete.

Then let us pray for the grace and protection of readiness. Let us pray that the gospel of peace may more and more deeply possess our souls, so that we may be inspired with that spontaneous readiness which awaits the King's bidding, and which speeds on its way carrying the glorious treasures of grace. "Have your feet shod with the readiness of the gospel of peace." "How beautiful upon the mountains are the feet of him that bringeth good tidings!"

V: THE SHIELD OF FAITH

Most Holy God, Who lightenest every man that cometh into the world, enlighten our hearts, we pray Thee, with the light of Thy grace, that we may fully know our sins and our shortcomings, and may confess them with true sorrow and contrition of heart. Unveil Thy love to us, so that in its clear shining we may behold the sin of our rebellion, and may turn unto Thee in humility and fervent devotion. Deliver us, we pray Thee, from the tyranny of evil habit. Save us from acknowledging any sovereignty above Thine. Keep us in sight of the great white throne, and may Thy judgments determine all our ways. Defend us when we are tempted to fields of transgression. Protect us from the allurements which assail the senses, and which entice us, through our fleshly desires, into impure delights. Loose us from the bonds of vanity and pride, and remove every perverting prejudice which blinds our vision. Impart unto us the grace of simplicity. May our worship be perfectly candid and sincere. Give us a healthy recoil from all hypocrisy, from all mere acting in Thy holy Presence. Quicken our perception that we may realize Thy Presence, and feel the awe of the unseen. Lead us, we pray Thee, to the fountain of life. Quicken our souls so that we may apprehend the things that concern our peace. Amen.

"Above all, taking the shield of faith, wherewith ye shall be able to quench all the fiery darts of the wicked." Ephesians 6:16.

But did the apostle who gives the counsel find his faith an all-sufficient shield? He recommends the shield of faith, but is the recommendation based on personal experience? And if so, what is the nature and value of that experience? What sort of protection did his faith give to him? When I examine his life what tokens do I find of guardianship and strong defence? When I move through the ways of his experience is it like passing through quiet and shady cloisters shut away from the noise and heat of the fierce and feverish world? Is his protected life like a garden walled around, full of sweet and pleasant things, and secured against the maraudings of robber and beast? Let us look at this protected life. Let us glance at the outer circumstances. Here is one glimpse of his experience: "Of the Jews five times received I forty stripes save one; once was I stoned; thrice have I suffered shipwreck; a day and a night have I been in the deep; in stripes above measure; in prisons more frequent; in deaths oft; in weariness and painfulness, in watchings often, in hunger and thirst, in fastings often, in cold and nakedness." And yet this is the man who speaks about the shield of faith, and in spite of the protecting shield all these things happened unto him!

Look at his bodily infirmities. "There was given unto me a thorn in the flesh." Where was the shield? It is not necessary for us to know the character of his thorn. But assuredly it was some ailment which appeared to interfere with the completeness of his work. Some think it was an affliction of the eyes; others think that it was a proneness to some form of malarial fever which frequently brought him into a state of collapse and exhaustion. But there it was, and the shield of faith did not keep it away.

Or look again at his exhausting labours. There is no word concerning his ministry more pregnant with meaning than this word "labour," which the apostle so frequently used to describe his work. "In labours oft;" "whereunto I labour;" "I laboured more abundantly than they all." This is not the labour of ordinary toil. It is the labour of travail. It is labour to the degree of poignant pang. It is labour that so expends the strength as to empty the fountain. It is the labour of sacrifice. And I thought that perhaps a protected life might have been spared the sufferings of a living martyrdom and that the service such a man rendered might have been made fruitful without pain. I thought God might have protected His servant. But the shield of faith did not deliver him from the labour of travail through which he sought the birth of the children of grace.

Or look once more at his repeated failures. You can hear the wail of sadness as he frequently contemplates his ruined hopes concerning little churches which he had built, or concerning fellow-believers whom he had won to Christ. "Are ye so soon fallen away?" "Ye would have given your eyes to me but now——." "I hear that there is strife among you." "It is reported that there is uncleanness among you." "Demas hath forsaken me." And it is wail after wail, for it is failure after failure. Defeat is piled upon defeat. It is declared to be a protected life, and yet disasters litter the entire way. It is perfectly clear that the shield of faith did not guard him from the agony of defeat.

Such are the experiences of the man who gave his strength to proclaim the all-sufficiency of the shield of faith, who spent his days in recommending it to his fellow-men, and whose own life was nevertheless noisy with tumult, and burdened with antagonisms, and crippled by infirmity, and clouded with defeat. Can this life be said to be wearing a shield? We have so far been looking at the man's environment, at his bodily infirmities, at his activities of labor, at his external defeats. What if in all these things we have not come within sight of the realm which the apostle would describe as his life? When Paul speaks of life he means the life of the soul. When he thinks of life his eyes are on the soul. In all the estimates and values which he makes of life he is fixedly regarding the soul. The question of success or failure in life is judged by him in the courthouse of the soul. You cannot entice the apostle away to life's accidents and induce him to take his measurements there. He always measures life with the measurement of an angel, and thus he busies himself not with the amplitude of possessions, but with the quality of being, not with the outer estates of circumstances but with the central keep and citadel of the soul. We never find the apostle Paul with his eyes glued upon the wealth or poverty of his surroundings. But everywhere and always and with endless fascination, he watches the growth or decay of the soul. When, therefore, this man speaks of the shield of faith we may be quite sure that he is still dwelling near the soul and that he is speaking of a protection which will defend the innermost life from foul and destructive invasion.

Now our emphasis is prone to be entirely the other way, and therefore we are very apt to misinterpret the teachings of the apostle Paul and to misunderstand the holy promises of the Lord. We are prone to live in the incidents of life rather than in its essentials, in environment rather than in character, in possessions rather than in dispositions, in the body rather than in the soul. The consequence is that we seek our shields in the realms in which we live. We live only in the things of the body and therefore against bodily ills we seek our shields. We want a shield against sorrow, to keep it away, a shield to protect us against the break-up of our happy estate. We want a shield against adversity, to keep it away, a shield against the darkening eclipse of the sunny day. We want a shield against loss, to keep it away, a shield against the rupture of pleasant relations, a shield to protect us against the bereavements which destroy the completeness of our fellowships. We want a shield against pain, to keep it away, a shield against the pricks and goads of piercing circumstances, against the stings and arrows of outrageous fortune.

In a word, we want a shield to make us comfortable, and because the shield of faith does not do it we are often stunned and confused, and our thin reasonings are often twisted and broken, and the world appears a labyrinth without a providence and without a plan. It is just here that our false emphasis leads us astray. We live in circumstances and seek a shield to make us comfortable; but the apostle Paul lived in character and sought a shield to make him holy. He was not concerned with the arrangement of circumstances, but he was concerned with the aspiration that, be the circumstances what they might, they should never bring disaster to his soul. He did not seek a shield to keep off ill-circumstances, but he sought a shield to keep ill-circumstances from doing him harm. He sought a shield to defend him from the destructiveness of every kind of circumstance, whether fair or foul, whether laden with sunshine or heavy with gloom. Paul wanted a shield against all circumstances in order that no circumstance might unman him and impoverish the wealth of his soul.

Let me offer a simple illustration. A ray of white light is made up of many colors, but we can devise screens to keep back any one of these colors and to let through those we please. We can filter the rays. Or we can devise a screen to let in rays of light and to keep out rays of heat. We can intercept certain rays and forbid their presence. Now, to the apostle Paul the shield of faith was a screen to intercept the deadly rays which dwell in every kind of circumstance; and to Paul the deadly rays in circumstances, whether the circumstances were bright or cloudy, were just those that consumed his spiritual susceptibilities and lessened his communion with God, the things that ate out his moral fibre, and that destroyed the wholeness and wholesomeness of his human sympathies, and impaired his intimacy with God and man. It was against these deadly rays he needed a shield, and he found it in the shield of faith.

Paul wanted a shield, not against failure; that might come or stay away. But he wanted a shield against the pessimism that may be born of failure, and which holds the soul in the fierce bondage of an Arctic winter. Paul wanted a shield, not against injury; that might come or stay away; but against the deadly thing that is born of injury, even the foul offspring of revenge. Paul wanted a shield, not against pain; that might come or might not come; he sought a shield against the spirit of murmuring which is so frequently born of pain, the deadly, deadening mood of complaint. Paul wanted a shield, not against disappointment, that might come or might not come; but against the bitterness that is born of disappointment, the mood of cynicism which sours the milk of human kindness and perverts all the gentle currents of the soul. Paul wanted a shield, not against difficulty; that might come or might not come; but against the fear that is born of difficulty, the cowardice and the disloyalty which are so often bred of stupendous tasks. Paul did not want a shield against success; that might come or might not come; but against the pride that is born of success, the deadly vanity and self-conceit which scorch the fair and gracious things of the soul as a prairie-fire snaps up a homestead or a farm. Paul did not want a shield against wealth; that might come or might not come; but against the materialism that is born of wealth, the deadly petrifying influence which turns flesh into stone, spirituality into benumbment, and which makes a soul unconscious of God and of eternity. The apostle did not want a shield against any particular circumstance, but against every kind of circumstance, that in everything he might be defended against the fiery darts of the devil.

He found the shield he needed in a vital faith in Christ. First of all the faith-life cultivates the personal fellowship of the Lord Jesus Christ. The ultimate concern of faith is not with a polity, not with a creed, not with a church, and not with a sacrament, but with the person of the Lord Jesus Christ. And therefore the first thing we have to do if we wish to wear the shield of faith is to cultivate the companionship of the Lord. We must seek His holy presence. We must let His purpose enter into and possess our minds. We must let His promises distil into our hearts. And we must let our own hearts and minds dwell upon the Lord Jesus in holy thought and aspiration, just as our hearts and minds dwell upon the loved ones who have gone from our side. We must talk to Him in secret and we must let Him talk to us. We must consult Him about our affairs, and then take His counsels as our statutes, and pay such heed to them that the statutes will become our songs. Faith-life cultivates the friendship of Christ, and leans upon it, and surrenders itself with glorious abandon to the sovereign decrees of His grace and love.

And then, secondly, the faith-life puts first things first, and in its list of primary values it gives first place to the treasures of the soul. Faith-life is more concerned with habits than with things, with character than with office, with self-respect than with popular esteem. The faith-life puts first things first, the clean mind and the pure heart, and from these it never turns its eyes away.

And, lastly, the faith-life contemplates the campaign rather than the single battle. One battle may seem to go against it. But faith knows that one battle is not the end of the world. "I will see you again, and your sorrow shall be turned into joy." Faith takes the long view, the view of the entire campaign. "I saw the holy city, the new Jerusalem, coming down out of heaven from God." "The kingdoms of this world shall become the kingdom of our God." Such a relationship to the Lord protects our life as with an invincible shield. It may please God to conduct our life through long reaches of cloudless noon; the shield of faith will be our defence. It may please God to lead us through the gloom of a long and terrible night; the shield of faith will be our defence. "Thou shalt not be afraid of the pestilence that walketh in darkness nor for the destruction that wasteth at noonday."

VI: THE HELMET OF HOPE

Eternal God, mercifully help us to unitedly draw near to the atoning Saviour, and through His mercies find access into the inheritance of the saints in light. Forgive the sins of our rebellion and redeem us from our guilt. Transform our spiritual habits that we may find ourselves able to fix our minds upon things above. Cleanse our hearts by the waters of regeneration, in order that our inclinations may be fixed upon the things that please Thee. Rekindle the fire of our affections, purify the light of our conscience. Broaden our compassions and make them more delicate in their discernments. Impart unto us the saving sense of Thy Companionship, and in the assurance of Thy Presence may we know ourselves competent to do Thy will. Meet with us one by one. Equip us with all needful armour for our daily battle. Feed us with hidden manna, that so our strength may be equal to our task. Unite us in the bonds of holy fear, and may we all be partakers of Thy love and grace. Amen.

"And take the helmet of salvation." Ephesians 6:17.

"And for an helmet the hope of salvation." I Thessalonians 5:8.

The helmet of hope! Who has not experienced the energy of a mighty hope? It is always a force to be reckoned with in the day of life's battle. Hope is a splendid helmet, firmly covering the head, and defending all its thoughts and purposes and visions from the subtle assaults of the evil one. The helmet of hope is one of the best protections against "losing one's head"; it is the best security against all attacks made upon the mind by small but deadly fears; it is the only effective safeguard against petty but deadly compromise. Far away the best defence against all sorts of mental vagrancy and distraction is to have the executive chambers of the life encircled and possessed by a strong and brilliant hope.

Now every student of the apostle Paul knows that he is an optimist. But he is an optimist, not because he closes his eyes, but because he opens them and uses them to survey the entire field of vision and possibility. He is an optimist, not because he cannot see the gross darkness,—no one has painted the darkness in blacker hues,—but because he can also see the light; and no one has portrayed the light with more alluring brilliance and glory. He is an optimist, not because he cannot see the loathsome presence of weakness, but because he sees the unutterable grace and love of God.

Yes, he is a reasonable optimist, and I dare to say that you cannot find anywhere in human literature a hundred pages more glowing and radiant with the spirit of hope than in the letters of the apostle Paul. Nowhere can you travel with him, not even to the darkest and most tragic realms of human need, without catching the bright shining of a splendid hope. You know how it is when you walk along the shore with the full moon riding over the sea. Between you and the moon, and right across the troubled waters, there is a broad pathway of silver light. If you move up the shore the shining path moves with you. If you move down the shore still you have the silver path across the waves. Wherever you stand there is always between you and the moon a shining vista stretching athwart the restless sea. And wherever the great apostle journeyed, and through whatever cold or desolate circumstances, there was always between him and the risen Lord, the Lord of grace and love, a bright and broadening way of eternal hope. No matter where he is, and how appalling the need, no matter what corruption may gather about the shore on which he is walking, always there is the silver path of gospel-hope stretching from the human shore-line to the burning bliss of the eternal Presence. In Jerusalem, in Antioch, in Lystra, in Ephesus, in Philippi, in Rome, he was never without these holy beams. They moved with him wherever he went, for they were the outshining rays of the mercy of the eternal God. Yes indeed, he was an optimist born and sustained in grace. He saw a shining road of hope out of every pit, stretching from the miry clay to the awful and yet glorious sanctities of holiness and peace.

Now our ordinary experience teaches us how much energy resides in a commanding hope. A big expectation is stored with wonderful dynamic, and it transmits its power to every faculty in the soul. The influence of a great hope fills the mind with an alert and sensitive trembling, inspiring every thought to rise as it were on tiptoe to await and greet the expected guest. A great hope pours its energy into the will, endowing it with the strength of marvellous patience and perseverance. I have lately read of an ingenious contrivance, which is now being used in some parts of Egypt, in which, by a subtle combination of glass receivers, the heat of the sun is collected, and the gathered energy concentrated and used in turning machinery in the varied ministries of agriculture. That is to say, the power of a diffused shining is directed to an engine and its strength enlisted in practical service. And so it is with the sunny light of a large hope. Its gathered energy is poured into the engine of the will, imparting glorious driving power, the power of "go" and laborious persistence.

Every sphere of human interest provides examples of this principle. Turn to the realm of invention. An inventor has a great hope shining before him as a brilliant vision of possible achievement. With what energy of will it endows him, and with what tireless, sleepless, invincible patience! Think of the immeasurable endurance of the brothers Wright who were inspired by the great hope of achieving the conquest of the air! Their hope was indeed a helmet defending them against all withering suggestions of ease, protecting them against the call of an ignoble indolence which is so often heard in hours of defeat. An electric railway has just been introduced by its inventor to the British Government, which is capable of transmitting mails and parcels along a prepared track at the rate of three hundred miles per hour; and the inventor has recently quietly told us that he has been at work upon it for thirty years! But think how, all through those long and many fruitless years, his helmet of hope defended him, and especially protected him from those alluring suggestions which come from the mild climate of Lotus-Land, and which tempt a man to relax his tension and lie down in the pleasant and thymy banks of rest and ease.

Or seek your examples in the realms of discovery. Read the chapters in Lord Lister's life which tell how he, braced and inspired by a mighty hope, laboured and laboured in the quest of an anæsthetic. Or turn to the equally fascinating pages which tell how Sir James Simpson toiled, and moiled, and dared, and suffered in the long researches which led to the discovery of chloroform. His will was rendered indomitable by the splendid hope of assuaging human pain.

Or think again of the restless, tireless labours of hundreds of men who are to-day engaged in searching for the microscopic cause of cancer, that having found it they might isolate it, and discover an antagonist which shall work its complete destruction. There is a glorious hope shining across the cancer waste, and it is nerving the will of research with unconquerable perseverance. Yes, indeed, men wear a splendid helmet, even in the ways of common experience, when they wear the helmet of hope.

And mark their condition when they lose it. Turn to the scriptural record of the voyage when Paul and his fellow-prisoners were being escorted by soldiers to take their trial in Rome: A tempestuous storm arose, and, in the power of a mighty hope to save the boat and themselves the men called out every ounce of their strength. But now note this connection in the narrative as I read it to you: "All hope was taken away." ... "We let her drift." That is it, and it offers a striking symbol of a common experience. While our hope is burning we steer; when our hope is gone out we drift. The motive power is gone, and the hopeless man is like a drifting hull in the midst of a wild and desolate sea.

Or turn to the pages of Capt. Scott's journal when he and his party are surmounting colossal tasks in the chivalrous hope of winning for their country the honourable distinction of first discovery of the South Pole. The narrative just blazes with hope, and therefore it tingles with energy and shouts with song! But when Amundsen's flag was seen at the Pole, and their strong hope was gone, and the disappointed company began to return—O what heavy feet, and what accumulated burdens, and what fiercely added laboriousness to an already laborious road! Hope had gone, and they nobly trudged, and trudged, and trudged, to faint, and fall, and die! Aye, men and women, hope is a tremendous power. To have hope is to have always fresh reserves to meet every new expenditure of the will. To lose hope is like losing the dynamo, the secret of inspiration, and the once indomitable will droops and faints away. It just makes an infinite difference whether or not we are wearing the helmet of hope.

But now, if all this is true of common hope and common experience, how is it with the supreme hope, "the hope of salvation?" What is this hope,—"the hope of salvation?" To whom is the apostle Paul giving this counsel? He is giving it to Christian believers in Ephesus: But were they not already saved? Why should he speak to them of "the hope of salvation" as though it were something still to be won? I remember when I was a mere boy going to Spurgeon's Tabernacle, and as I was retiring from the building at the close of the service, a gentleman laid his hand upon my shoulder, and said: "My boy, are you saved?" His question suggested that it was something I might already have experienced. Well, had not the Ephesian disciples passed through that same experience? A little while ago a London cabman stood at the foot of the pulpit-stairs in our church, and told me that by the grace of God he had been wonderfully saved. But the apostle speaks to these believers of "the hope of salvation" as though it were something still before them. They had taken a great step in discipleship in that vast and wicked city of Ephesus, crowded with all sorts of antagonisms, and they had boldly confessed themselves on the side of Christ. And yet, the apostle counsels them to wear as a helmet "the hope of salvation."

The truth is that the apostle Paul uses all the three primary tenses in speaking of salvation. He speaks to believers in the past tense, and he says: "We were saved." And to the same believers he uses the present tense, and he says: "Ye are being saved." And yet again to the same believers he uses the future tense, "Ye shall be saved." All of which means that to this great apostle a gloriously full salvation stretches across the years from past to future, gathering riches with every passing day. Salvation to Paul was more than a step, it was also a walk. It was more than a crisis, it was also a prolonged process. It was more than the gift of new life, it was the maturing in growth and power. A drowning man, when he is lifted out of the water, is in a very profound sense vitally saved. But after this initial salvation there is the further salvation of re-collecting his scattered consciousness, and of recovering his exhausted strength. And in a very glorious sense a man is spiritually saved in a moment; in a moment in Christ Jesus he passed from death into life. But it is also equally true that a man is only saved in a lifetime, as he appropriates to himself more and more the grace and truth of the risen Lord. Yes, after we have been converted and saved, there is a further salvation in self-recovery, in self-discovery, all of which becomes ours in a fuller and richer discovery of Christ. Our possibilities of salvation in Christ Jesus stretch before us like range upon range of glorious mountains. When we have attained one range we have only obtained a new vantage-ground for beholding another; when that, too, has been climbed, still vaster and grander ranges rise into view. Every fresh addition to our Christlikeness increases our power of discernment, and every added power of discernment unfolds a larger vision and a more glorious and alluring hope. All believers in Christ Jesus have been saved. All believers in Christ Jesus are being saved. All believers in Christ Jesus will be saved. And therefore, says the apostle, always wear the helmet of hope, "the hope of salvation."

Now perhaps we cannot better draw this meditation to a close in more immediate and practical purpose than by just gazing upon one or two of the hopes of the apostle Paul, if perchance by God's good grace we may appropriate them to our own souls. For he, too, is wearing the helmet of hope, the hope of salvation. What, then, does he hope for? What mighty hope is throwing the energies of its defences upon and around his soul? Here is one of his hopes; look at it: "In hope of the glory of God." He wore that hope, and he wore it like a helmet, and he wore it night and day. He had gazed upon the glory of the Lord, the wondrous light of grace and truth which shone in the face of Jesus Christ. And now he dared to hold the glorious hope of becoming glorified with the same glory. He dared to hope that his own soul would become translucent with the holy light of divine truth and purity. It almost makes one catch the breath to see such spiritual audacity. One has read of young boys trembling with artistic sensibility, bowing in the presence of the world's masterpieces in art or music, and becoming possessed with the amazing hope of one day sharing the master's light and glory. But here is a man who has been prostrate in the presence of his God. He has been humbly gazing upon "the chief among ten thousand and the altogether lovely." And now, in a daring which yet quiets the soul in reverence and prayerful lowliness, he tells his fellow-believers that he lives "in hope of the glory of God." What a hope! The hope of being glorified with God's glory, of being made gracious with His grace, of being made truthful with His truth, of being sanctified with His holiness, of being transformed into the same image, from glory unto glory! I say, what a hope, and therefore, what a helmet! With a helmet like that defending a man's brain, what a defence he has against all the petty devilries which seek to enter among our thoughts in the shape of mean purposes, and petty moral triflings, such as so often invade and desolate the whole realm of the mind! What a hope this is, and what a helmet; "the hope of the glory of God."

And here is another way the apostle has of describing the hope he wears, "the hope of salvation;"—"To present us spotless before His throne." Quietly and reverently repeat that phrase, again, and again, and again, until something of its grandeur begins to fill your soul as the advancing light of the rising sun fills a vale in Switzerland with its soft and mellowing glory. "To present us spotless before His throne." What a hope! And yet this man wore it every day, in all the ups and downs, the victories and defeats of his ever-changing life. "To present us spotless before His throne!" Just think of wearing that hope in New York! And by God's good grace we can wear it; yes, indeed, we can, and what a helmet to wear! When a man has got that helmet on, and some sharp temptation is hurled at him, it will fall away from him like a paper pellet thrown against the armour plate of a mighty dreadnought. "To present us spotless!" Wear that helmet of hope, and the devil shall batter thee in vain. For what can the devil do with men and women in whom these hopes are blazing? He offers us his glittering snares, and they are revealed as common paste in the presence of genuine stones. They stand exposed as noisy fireworks in the presence of the stars.

Let us wear the helmet of hope, the helmet of salvation, and we are quite secure. But let us put it on every day. Every morning let us put on the helmet, and often and again during the day let us feel that it is in its place. Let us begin the day by saying, "Now, my soul, live to-day in hope of the glory of God! Live to-day in the hope of being presented spotless before His throne! Live to-day in the hope of being 'filled unto all the fulness of God'." Let us put that helmet on, and let us do it deliberately, prayerfully, and trustfully, and in life's evil day we shall be able to stand, and having done all, to stand.

VII: THE SWORD OF THE SPIRIT

Heavenly Father, Who hast given Thy Holy Spirit to comfort and to guide Thy servants, teach us to trust His leading. Day by day we would listen to His consolation and direction. When we open Thy Word of Life we would rely upon His illuminating interpretation. When the story of the character and the depths of the teaching of Jesus are far beyond us, and seem unapproachable, when doubts and fears assail the mind, let us abide in quiet repose under the tuition of the indwelling Spirit. When desire for the highest life fails, and hunger and thirst after righteousness are forgotten in other pursuits, may the kindly Spirit inspire afresh the ardor of enthusiasm which He alone can create. When we have lost our bearings in the maze of life teach us to look to the ever-present Guide Who brings back into the clear path all Who trust Him; through Jesus Christ. Amen.

"Take the sword of the Spirit which is the Word of God." Ephesians 6:17.

Here is the Christian soldier with his sword, and his sword is the Word of God. And what a sword it is! "Then said Mr. Greatheart to Mr. Valiant-for-truth, Thou hast worthily behaved thyself; let me see thy sword. So he showed it him. When he had taken it into his hand and looked thereon a while, he said, Ha, it is a right Jerusalem blade. Then said Mr. Valiant-for-truth, It is so. Let a man have one of these blades, with a hand to wield it, and skill to use it, and he may venture upon an angel with it. He need not fear its holding if he can but tell how to lay on. Its edge will never blunt. It will cut flesh and bones, and soul and spirit and all." Yes indeed, this sword is a serviceable and most efficient weapon. And it might be profitable, in the very beginning of our meditation, to go on to the field of actual battle and watch one or two mighty swordsmen wielding the sword in actual war. And let us begin with Him who could wield the sword as none other could do and who never drew it in vain. "And the tempter came to Him and said, If Thou art the Son of God command that these stones be made bread." At once the Master's hand was on the hilt of His sword and He drew it forth for combat. "It is written man shall not live by bread alone." It was "the sword of the Spirit, which is the Word of God!" [The place of battle is now changed, but the missing text] unto Him, "All these things will I give Thee if Thou wilt fall down and worship me." And again the Master whipped out His sword;—"Get thee hence, Satan, for it is written, Thou shalt worship the Lord Thy God, and Him only shalt Thou serve." It was "the sword of the Spirit which is the Word of God!"

Now turn your eyes to quite another field of battle where one of the Master's disciples, a very skilful swordsman, is in combat with a very deadly foe. "And when the people saw what Paul had done"—he had just given a cripple the power to walk—"they lifted up their voices saying, The gods are come down to us in the likeness of men. And they called Barnabas Jupiter, and Paul Mercurius, because he was the chief speaker." Now what did the apostle do in the presence of so deadly a peril, a peril which garbed itself in the attractive robes of light? Immediately he drew out his sword, and fought his shining antagonist with a word from the 146th Psalm! That is excellent swordwork, by a most excellent swordsman! And he used "the sword of the Spirit which is the Word of God."

Or turn once more to another field of battle, to the Valley of Humiliation, where "poor Christian was hard put to it. For he had gone but a little way before he espied a foul fiend coming over the field to meet him; his name was Apollyon." "Then did Christian draw, for he saw it was time to bestir him; Apollyon as fast made at him, throwing darts as thick as hail.... The sword combat lasted for about half a day, even till Christian was almost quite spent; for you must know that Christian, by reason of his wounds, must needs grow weaker and weaker. Then Apollyon, espying his opportunity, began to gather up close to Christian, and wrestling with him gave him a dreadful fall; and with that Christian's sword flew out of his hand. Then said Apollyon, I am sure of thee now. And with that he had almost pressed him to death, so that Christian began to despair of life. But as God would have it, while Apollyon was fetching his last blow, thereby to make a full end of this good man, Christian nimbly reached out his hand for his sword, saying, Rejoice not against me, oh mine enemy: when I fall I shall arise; and with that gave him a deadly thrust which made him give back as one that had received his mortal wound. Christian perceiving that made at him again, saying, 'Nay, in all these things we are more than conquerors through Him that loved us.' And with that Apollyon spread forth his broken wings, and sped him away, so that Christian saw him no more.... I never saw Christian all this while give as much as one pleasant look, till he perceived he had wounded Apollyon with his two-edged sword; then indeed he did smile and look upward.... Then there came to him a man with some of the leaves of the tree of life, the which Christian took and applied to the wounds that he had received in the battle and was healed immediately." Surely to watch expert fighters like these, who turn their battlefields into fields of glory, makes one more ambitious to possess and wield that same two-edged sword, the sword of the Spirit which is the Word of God!

Well now, it is this sword which Paul advises these young disciples at Ephesus to get and hold at all costs, and never to leave it rusting in the scabbard at home. And surely, if there was need for swordwork anywhere it was in that gay, shallow, materialistic city of Ephesus. We have been reading many terrible accounts of late of bayonet fighting in the trenches in Belgium and France, where gunnery attacks were unavailable, and where men came face to face in the hot breath of one another's passions, and were locked in the death-grip of hand-to-hand encounter. It was even so with the spiritual warfare in Ephesus. There was no long-range fighting, no far distant antagonisms, no remote or merely theoretical persecution. The foes of the soul were exceedingly real, exceedingly near, and exceedingly intimate. In Ephesus your enemy was upon you in a moment, and there was nothing for it but never to let the sword fall from your hand. Spiritual enemies approached the soul every hour of the day, and it was imperative to run them through with the sword of the truth. There were falsities, and subtleties, and evasions; there were ambiguities and sophistries; there were half truths linked with black falsehood, and white lies linked with snatches of truth; there were exaggerations and perversions; there were insinuations and evil counsels; there were mean expediencies and illicit compromises; there were hypocrisies of every kind in that prosperous city of Ephesus, tricked out in apparent seemliness, and perilous in all the wiles of the devil. What, then, was a young Christian to do in all that immoral welter? He must have his sword in hand, always in hand, and he must prick these bubbles, and pierce these showy disguises, and rend these deceptive veils, and he must do it at once, before they mastered him with the plausible counterfeits of the truth.

I saw a photograph the other day from the European field of war, in which a company of soldiers were examining a load of hay. They were piercing it with their swords in the endeavour to find out if any foe lay hidden in the fragrant pile. And I could not but think of the warfare of the soul, and of the sweet and fragrant disguises in which the devil is so often concealed. The devil in a hay-rick! I have experienced it a thousand times. A deadly temptation hidden in some innocent expediency! Some fatal lure concealed in a popular custom! Corruption housing itself in a white lie! The enemy wearing a white robe! The devil, I say, in a hay-rick! In such conditions there was only one resource for these disciples in Ephesus, as there is only one resource for you and me to-day, to have our swords always ready, and to pierce these glistening falsities in the blessed name of the holy and unchanging God. Yes, whip out your sword, the sword of the Spirit, which is the Word of God.

What, then, is this sword? It is "the Word of God." And what is this Word of God which we are to flash through all falsehood like the thrust of a gleaming sword? What is this Word which is to be our sword? Well, first of all, it is the word of divine truth; God's way of thinking about things. And therefore when we are wielding the sword we are using a thought of God. We are to use God's thought about a thing in fighting all other thoughts about that thing. For instance, we are to take God's thought about life, and use it as a sword to meet and destroy all mean and unworthy conceptions of life. We are to take God's thought about sin and use it in combating all the lax and deadly conceptions of sin which are so loose and rampant in our own day. We are to take God's thought about holiness, and use it in fighting all ignoble compromises which may satisfy a poor standard in the kingdom of the letter, but which have no standing in the more glorious realm of the spirit. We are to take God's thought about worship, and fight all the little, mean, seductive ritualisms which so frequently strut about in royal and gorgeous robes, but which are empty of all vital spiritual wealth and power.

And so with a thousand other relations. God's thought about a thing is to be our sword in fighting all the debasing thoughts of that thing; it may be God's thought of work, or of wealth, or of success, or of failure, or God's thought of pleasure, or of service, or of death. What does God think about a thing? That is my sword, the thought of God which is the word of God. And we are to take that shining, flaming, flashing thought, and use it as a sword among all the creeping, crawling things, or against all the flying and bewitching subtleties of things which abounded in Ephesus, and which are equally prolific in London or New York. And so does the apostle give us this counsel: "Take the sword of the spirit, which is the thought or word of God."

And now I can add a second characteristic of the sword, a characteristic which amplifies and corroborates the first. This word of God, which is to be our sword, is not only the word of divine truth as laid upon the mind. It is also the word of divine commandment as laid upon the will. It is a word which divinely reveals our personal duty, imposing upon us some imperative mission. Some word of God comes to us with the mysterious suggestion of obligation, and we often receive it over against some soft and wooing temptation to an indulgent indolence; and we are to take the divine word of obligation, and with it fight and slay the soft seduction to ease.

We have this sort of warfare most vividly described in the experience of the prophet Jonah. Let me set it before you. "And the word of the Lord came unto Jonah, saying, Arise, go to Nineveh, that great city, and cry against it!" Let us note the lines of this experience. The word of the Lord came to Jonah as an imperative and an obligation. It said "Nineveh!" But another word came to Jonah, a soft, luxurious, seductive word, luring him to Tarshish. And there you have all the conditions of spiritual warfare; and the only way for the believer is to take the word of obligation, and use it as a mighty sword against the word of seduction; he must take his sword and slay it, or chase it in miserable flight from the field. The word of duty is the word of God, and therefore the word of duty is thy sword against every plausible temptation that would snare thee to disloyal ease.

There is still a third descriptive word about the sword, and which again corroborates and enriches the others. The word of God, which is the sword of the spirit, is not only the word of divine truth laying God's thought upon the mind; and not only the word of divine commandment laying God's purpose upon the will; it is also the word of divine promise laying God's strengthening comfort upon the heart. Just think of that fine sword, the word of promise, being handed to these young and tempted disciples in this awful, hostile city of Ephesus. I think we may easily imagine, without presumption, how they would apply the apostle's counsel, and how the older men among them would train the younger men in the expert use of this shining sword. They would say: "Whenever you go out to your work, amid all the cold, bristling antagonisms of the world, carry the sword of promise! When your circumstances seem to mock you because of your unnerving loneliness, whip out the sword of promise! When you appear to be in a minority of one, and the enemy swarms in menace around you on every side, carry this sword of promise in your right hand, 'I will never leave thee nor forsake thee.' And when the enemy taunts you because of your weakness, or your want of culture, or your lack of rank and social prestige, or your nobodyism and nothingism, whip out the sword and fight the taunt with this word of promise, 'Neither shall any one pluck you out of my hand'!" Thus do I think these disciples would speak to one another, as, blessed be God, disciples can speak to one another to-day. When the devil comes to us in our loneliness, in our weakness, in our seeming abandonment, let us lay hold of the word of grace, and fight all the enemies' taunts with the divine promise, and pierce them through and through, turning the foe to rout, and remaining more than conquerors on the hard and finely won field.

Well, such is what I think to be the sword. It is the word of divine truth, it is the word of divine commandment, and it is the word of divine promise. It is a superlatively excellent sword, "it is a right Jerusalem blade." "Let a man have one of these blades, with a hand to wield it, and skill to use it, and he may venture upon an angel with it." Its edge will never blunt, for it is "the sword of the spirit, which is the word of God."

Where, then, can we find this word of God which is to be our sword of the spirit. Well, first of all, we can find the word of God in the sacred Scriptures. We can get our sword from its splendid armoury. Here is the word which gives the revelation of truth, telling me how the great God thinks about things, and therefore, telling me how to think amid all the plausible errors of our time. And here, too, is the word which gives the revelation of duty, telling me what the great God would have me do. And here also is the word which gives the revelation of promise, telling me what resources are prepared for them who follow the fair gleams of truth and take the divine road of duty and obedience. Yes, the word of God is in the old Book, and here you can find your sword.

But sometimes the word of God is given to us, not through the medium of a book, not even the book of the Scriptures, but in a direct and immediate message to our own souls. Oh, yes, sometimes the Captain of our salvation gives me my sword without my having to make recourse to the written word. He speaks to me and hands me my sword with no intermediary between us. The word of the Lord comes unto thee and unto me as it came to the herdman Amos, and the courtier Isaiah, and to the fisherman Peter, and to the university student Paul. He speaks to thee and to me. "Hath He not promised, and shall He not do it"? "Thine ears shall hear a word behind thee, saying, This is the way; walk ye in it."

"And His that gentle voice we hear,
Soft as the breath of even;
That checks each fault, and calms each fear,
And speaks of heaven!"

If the sword of the spirit is the word of God, then sometimes I take my sword immediately from my Sovereign's hand,—the word of truth, the word of duty, and the word of promise,—and like St. Francis of Assisi, and St. Catherine of Sienna, and George Fox, all of them mystics, and all of them deep in the knowledge of the mind and heart of God, I, too, can take the sword and use it on the wide and changing battlefields of life, and be more than conqueror through Him Who loved me and gave Himself for me. "Take the sword of the spirit, which is the word of God."

Well, then, let us take the sword; let us draw it, and let us use it. Let us reverently find the word in the Book of Holy Writ, or in the secret chamber of our own soul; and then let us carry it as our sword to the immediate occasion, and to the next stage upon life's road. Let us have the sword ready, always ready; let us be always at attention, waiting with the word of God to meet the tempting word of man. A man without a sword is in a sorry way when the devil leaps upon him. That was the tragic plight of Judas Iscariot. When the chief priests and scribes came to bargain with him, to induce him to sell his Lord, he ought to have had his sword ready, and to have run it through the devilish suggestion when it was only newly born. But somehow, somehow, he had lost his sword, and he was undone—"and he covenanted with them for thirty pieces of silver"!

And when you and I are tempted to sell the Lord, when we are tempted to make a dirty bargain of any kind, when we are tempted to prefer money to integrity, or unholy ease to stern duty, or soft flattery to rugged truth, let us have our swords in our hands,—"the sword of the spirit which is the word of God"—and let us slay the suggestion at its very birth. Have your sword ready. You may need it before you get home. Have your sword ready! Fight the good fight of faith, and lay hold on eternal life.

VIII: THE SOLDIER'S USE OF PRAYER

Almighty God, Our Father, it is by Thy grace that we attain unto holiness, and it is by Thy light that we find wisdom. We humbly pray that Thy grace and light may be given unto us, so that we may come into the liberty of purity and truth. Wilt Thou graciously exalt our spirits and enable us to live in heavenly places in Christ Jesus? Impart unto us a deep dissatisfaction with everything that is low, and mean, and unclean, and create within us such pure desire that we may appreciate the things which Thou hast prepared for them that love Thee. Wilt Thou receive us as guests of Thy table? Give us the glorious sense of Thy presence, and the precious privilege of intimate communion. Feed us with the bread of life; nourish all our spiritual powers; help us to find our delight in such things as please Thee. Give us strength to fight the good fight of faith. Give us holy courage, that we may not be daunted by any fear, or turn aside from our appointed task. Make us calm when we are to tread an unfamiliar road, and may Thy presence give us companionship divine. Meet with us, we humbly pray Thee, in all the appointed means of grace, and may the joyful remembrance of this service inspire us in all common life and service of after days. Amen.

"Praying always with all prayer and supplication in the Spirit, and watching thereunto with all perseverance and supplication for all saints; and for me that utterance may be given unto me, that I may open my mouth boldly, to make known the mystery of the gospel." Ephesians 6:18, 19.

We have been engaged in studying the different pieces of the Christian soldier's armour as it is described to us by the apostle Paul. Let us now glance at the warrior as he stands before us fully armed and ready for the field. His loins are girt about with truth, the truth revealed in Jesus Christ our Lord. He is protected back and front with a coat of mail, the righteousness of the Lord Jesus, a righteousness which covers him in a moment as with a garment, and then little by little imparts to him the holy likeness of his Lord. His feet are shod with readiness, and are swiftly obedient to do the King's bidding and to carry his message of grace and good-will. He bears the shield of faith, his sure screen from every deadly dart springing from any kind of circumstance, whether in the cloudless noon or in the blackest midnight. On his head there is the helmet of salvation, the helmet of a mighty hope, protecting his mind from the invasion of deadly distractions, and from all the belittling suggestions of the evil one. In his hand he carries the sword of the Spirit, the word or thought of God, the shining thought wherewith every other kind of thought is overthrown or put to utter rout.

Now that, surely, is a brave and gleaming equipment. Surely the armour is all-sufficient, and the well-appointed, well-defended warrior is now ready for the field! Let him go forth to meet the great enemy of souls. Let him encounter all the wiles of the devil, and let him so hold himself and so use himself as to convert every hour of opportunity into a season of spiritual glory. No, no, not yet! Says the apostle, "Steady!" With all his shining armour his equipment is not yet complete. There is one other vital thing to be named, and this the Christian warrior must take along with him, for his warfare will be hopeless if he leaves it behind. "Praying always with all prayer and supplication in the Spirit, and watching thereunto with all perseverance and supplication for all saints."

Now why should the Christian warrior pray? He must pray as a suppliant for the robust health of his own spirit. Yes, but why should he pray for the maintenance of his own spiritual health? What is the vital relationship between the praying soul and the attainment of moral and spiritual robustness? How is prayer related to a man's moral force? This is the relationship. A praying warrior receives into his soul the grace-energies of the eternal God. The power of grace is just the holy love and strength and beauty of the holy Godhead flowing into the needs of the soul and filling them with its own completeness. Now we do not pray in order to make God willing to impart this grace, but in order to fit ourselves to receive it. We do not pray to ingratiate God's good-will, but to open our souls in hospitality. We do not pray in order to create a friendly air, but to let it in, not to propitiate God but to appropriate Him. We do not pray to turn a reluctant God toward ourselves, but to turn our reluctant selves toward a ready and bountiful God.

It is imperative that we should lay hold of this teaching very firmly. It is of the utmost moment we should know what we are doing when we pray for the bracing and sanctifying energies of the Holy Spirit. Prayer then, I say, is first and chiefly the establishment of communion with God. Prayer is the clearing of the blocked roads which are crowded with all sorts of worldly hindrances. Prayer is the preparing of the way of the Lord. When I turn to the Lord in prayer I open the doors and windows of my soul toward the heavenlies, and I open them for the reception of any gifts of grace which God's holy love may wish me to receive. My reverent thought in prayer perfects communion between my soul and God.

Let me offer an illustration. I am told there is electricity in my house. I am told that this mysterious, invisible, electric spirit is waiting to be my minister and to serve me in a dozen different ways. I go into a room where the genius is said to be waiting, and yet the room is held in darkness. Where is this friendly spirit? Where is the light which is one of its promised services? And then I am told that an action of mine, quite a simple one, is required, and that when the action has been performed the waiting spirit will reveal itself in radiant beams. And so I bring my will into play, and I push a button, or I lift a tiny lever, and my action completes the circuit, and the subtle energy leaps into the carbon filament and turns my darkness into light.

That is it! My action completes the circuit! And when I turn my will to pray, when I seek the holy, sanctifying power of God, my prayer completes the circuit between my soul and God, and I receive whatever the inexhaustible fountain of grace is always waiting to bestow. And so do I say that prayer is first of all, and most of all, the establishing of a vital communion between the soul and God.

Lord Tennyson, in what must have been a wonderful conversation on the subject of prayer with Mr. Gladstone, and Holman Hunt, and James Addington Symonds, said that to him prayer was the opening of the sluice-gates between his soul and the waters of eternal life. It is worth while just to dwell upon Tennyson's figure for a moment. The figure may have been taken from a canal. You enter a lock and you are shut up within its prison. And then you open the sluice-gates, and the water pours into your prison and lifts you up to the higher level, and your boat emerges again on a loftier plane of your journey.

Or the figure may have been taken from a miller's wheel: There are the miller and his mill. And the wheel is standing idle, or it is running but sluggishly and wearily at its work. And then the miller opens the sluice-gate, and the waiting water rushes along, and leaps upon the wheel, and makes it sing in the bounding rapidity of its motion. Prayer, says Tennyson, is the opening of the sluice-gates and the letting into the soul of the waiting life and power of God. Prayer opens the sluice-gates, and the water of life floods the sluggish affections, and freshens the drowsy sympathies, and braces and speeds the will like the glorious rush of the stream upon the miller's wheel.

That, to me, is the dominant conception of prayer. Prayer opens the soul to God. Prayer opens the life to the workings of infinite grace. And now I see why the Christian soldier should be so urgently counselled to pray. Prayer keeps open his lines of communication. Prayer keeps him in touch with his base of supplies. Without prayer he is isolated by the flanking movements of the world, the flesh, and the devil, and he will speedily give out in the dark and cloudy day. "Men ought always to pray and not to faint."

If that is one reason why the Christian soldier should pray in order to maintain the bounding health of his own spirit, we are now faced with the second question as to when he should pray. And here is the answer of the veteran warrior Paul: "Praying always." Not at some time, but at all times! "Praying always." But can we do that? "Always"? But I am called upon to earn my daily bread. I have to face a hundred different problems. Every bit of gray matter in my brain is devoting its strength to the immediate task. Is it possible for us to think of two things at once? Can we be thinking out some absorbing question in business, and at the same time be praying to God? One thing is surely perfectly clear, we cannot always be thinking of God: It is constitutionally impossible.

But now, while we cannot always be thinking of God, and always speaking to God, we can always be mentally disposed toward Him, so that whatever we are doing there can be a mental leaning or bias towards His most holy will. Let me show you what I mean. We must reverently dare to reason in this great matter as we reason in other relationships. Turn, then, for an illustration, to common gymnastics. In physical gymnastics there is no need for us to be always exercising, to be at it every moment of the waking day. The body does not need it. Indeed, it would resent it, and rebel against it. But here is the healthy genius of gymnastic exercises. Regular exercises give the body a certain healthy pose, a certain vigour and excellence of carriage, which the body retains between the exercises when we are going about our accustomed work. That is to say, conscious exercise makes unconscious habit. Our conscious exercise forces the body into attitudes which persist as habits when we are doing something else. We can retain the pose of the gymnasium on the street, and we can retain it without thinking.

And so it is with spiritual exercises when they are as real as the exercises in the gymnasium. When a man prays, and prays as deliberately and purposely as he practices physical exercises, when he drills his soul as he drills his body, he gives his mind and soul a certain pose, a certain attitude, a certain stateliness and loftiness of carriage. He gives his soul a healthy bias towards

God, and the soul retains the bias when he is no longer upon his knees. His soul carries itself Godward even when he is earning his daily bread. God can get at him any time and anywhere! The way is open, the communion is unbroken!

That is the vital logic of the matter. By regular spiritual exercises we can subdue the soul to spiritual habit. Again and again throughout the day it is possible for us, by a conscious upward glance, to confirm the habit; until it happens that the soul is always in the posture of prayer,—in business, in laughter, in trade, at home, or abroad, always in prayer,—and therefore, in every part of the wide and varied battleground of life receiving the all-sufficient grace and love of God. And so the Christian soldier is to be "Praying always, with all prayer and supplication in the spirit."

But the Christian soldier is not only a suppliant for his own spiritual health. He is much more than this. The apostle counsels him to be a suppliant for the health of the entire Christian army. "Praying always, with all prayer and supplication in the spirit, and watching thereunto with all perseverance and supplication for all saints." That is to say, the Christian soldier not only prays for the health of his own spirit, but for a healthy "esprit de corps" throughout the whole militant Church of Christ. It is his duty and privilege to be prayerfully jealous for all the saints, and for the spiritual equipment of all his fellow-soldiers on the field.

Now this is a very wonderful privilege entrusted to the disciple of Christ. To every believer there is entrusted the marvellous ministry of helping others to receive the energies of divine grace, and to strengthen them in the fierce combats of their own "evil day." For the character of our evil days is very varied. Your evil day may not be mine, and my evil day may not be yours. What makes an evil day for you may never trouble me, and what makes my day difficult and tempestuous may leave you perfectly serene. It is to be accounted for in many ways. The differences in our circumstances account, to some extent, for the differences in our evil days. The differences in our occupations create great differences in our daily warfare in the spirit. The differences in our temperaments make no two persons' battles quite alike. And yet, with all our differences, we are all called upon to stand in our own evil day, "and having done all, to stand." Peter's evil day would be very different from John's. Thomas' evil day would be very different from Nathanael's. Dorcas' evil day would be quite different to the evil days which gloomed upon Euodia and Synteche. But blessed be God, by the holy ministry of prayer we can strengthen one another to "stand in the evil day." We can help every soldier to keep his spiritual roads open and to prepare the way of the Lord. We are called upon to be sentinel suppliants on their behalf, "watching thereunto with all perseverance and supplication for all saints." We are to be ever on the look-out, vigilant for the entire army of the Lord, divinely jealous for its healthy spirit, and seeking for every man in the ranks the grace and glory which we seek for ourselves. What a magnificent man this true soldier of the Lord must be!

And then, just to finish it all, and by one example to show us how deep and wide is this ministry of supplication, the apostle Paul asks the young Ephesian soldiers to pray for him. "And for me, that utterance may be given unto me." Let us carefully note this, and let us observe its heartening significance. These young, immature Christians in Ephesus, trembling in their early faith, are asked to pray for the old warrior in Rome. He is now "an ambassador in bonds," held in captivity in imperial Rome, and the young soldiers in Ephesus are asked to be sentinel-suppliants for the stricken soldier far away. Do you believe this? And what does he want them to pray for? Listen to him again. "And for me, that utterance may be given unto me." Have you got the real inwardness of that appeal? A poor slave in Ephesus may, by his own prayer, anoint the lips of a great apostle with grace and power. What a vista of powerful possibility! Do all congregations realize that privilege and service concerning their ministers? "For me, that utterance may be given unto me." Do I realize that my prayers, obscure and nameless though I be, can give utterance to a Paul, a Livingstone, a Moffatt, or a Chalmers? Do I realize that I can pour grace upon their lips? What a brave and splendid privilege! Am I using it? I cannot get out of my mind the vision of some poor slave in Ephesus pouring grace and truth upon the apostle's lips in Rome, and I cannot get out of my imagination the surprise which awaited the slave in glory, when Paul asked him, as a fellow-labourer, to share in gathering in the sheaves.

"And for me, that utterance may be given unto me, that I may open my mouth boldly." And can we do that for a man, and do it by prayer? Can one soldier give another soldier nerve, and can he do it by prayer? Can he chase away his fears? Can he change timidity into pluck? Can he transform a lamb into a lion? What a marvellous power has God given to me and thee! The unbounded privilege of it all! Some slave in Ephesus giving new boldness to Paul in Rome, and enabling Paul to take some new ground and conquer it for the Lord! And once again I say, to be called to share in the apostle's triumphs! If any one has prayed for me, your fellow-soldier, that utterance and courage may be given unto me, and if by my ministry some depressed and retreating soldier finds heart again, and takes up his fallen sword, and fights anew the good fight, then that suppliant shall share my holy conquest in the Lord, and the joy of the Lord shall be his strength.

So once again, let us hear the apostle's counsel, and keep it in our hearts. "Praying always with all prayer and supplication in the Spirit, and watching thereunto with all perseverance and supplication for all saints; and for me, that utterance may be given unto me, that I may open my mouth boldly, to make known the mysteries of the gospel."

IX: "WATCH YE!"

Eternal God, we bow before Thee as the children of grace and love. Purify our souls, make our eyes keen and watchful, in order that we may discern Thy purpose at every turning of the way. Help us to hallow all our circumstances whether they appear friendly or adverse, and may we subdue them all to the King's will. We pray that we may obtain new visions of the glory of Christ. May His gospel of grace become more exceedingly precious as we gaze into its unsearchable wealth. Let in the light as our eyes are able to bear it. Tell us some of the many things which are yet withholden because we are not able to bear them. May we exercise our senses in discernment, that so we may be led into the deeper secrets of Thy truth. And wilt Thou graciously grant unto us new possibilities of service. May we light lamps on many a dark road. May we give help to many a tired pilgrim who is burdened by the greatness of the way. May we give cups of refreshment to those who are thirsty and faint. And may our own faith and hope restore the flickering light where courage is nearly spent. Amen.

"Watch ye, stand fast in the faith, quit you like men, be strong." I Corinthians 16:13.

This is the counsel of a brave warrior, experienced and weather-beaten, writing to raw and comparatively untried recruits. One is reminded of the veteran Lord Roberts when he lately spake to young English recruits who had not yet been baptized in the actual flames of battle, advising them about their own warfare of the spirit, and counselling them on no account to forfeit their self-respect and self-control. And this tried warrior, Paul, is addressing a little company of Christian recruits in the city of Corinth. Corinth is now wiped out, buried in the accumulated débris of the centuries. Here and there an excavated column bears desolate witness to the glory of former days, but Corinth as a city is sealed up in an unknown grave. But just behind the site of the city there appears the Acrocorinthius, rising to the height of two thousand feet. I climbed this famous hill in the spring because I wanted to see the panorama on which the apostle had gazed, and also to see the setting and relations of this once imperial city. It was a wonderful vision of natural glory, with deep, far-stretching valleys, and distant gleams of the sea, and range upon range of hills, many of them snow-covered and glistening in the blazing sunshine of a splendid noon. There below was the plain on which Corinth found her shelter, and beyond the plain the narrow water-way, which gave her such intimate relations with the commerce of the Mediterranean; and beyond the water-way there is a touch of old romance, for there rise the shrines of the muses, the twin peaks of Helicon and Parnassus.

Standing on this elevated eminence I tried to realize the conditions in which this little company of Christian recruits had to live the consecrated life. They had to fight the Christian warfare amid the soft luxuriousness of Corinth, a luxuriousness which relaxed the moral fibre, and made the Corinthians conspicuous for their depravity, "even amid all the depraved cities of a dying heathenism." Corinth was a city of abyssmal profligacy; "it was the Vanity Fair of the Roman Empire, at once the London and Paris of the ancient world"! And it was in this city, away there on the plain before me, that these untried Christian recruits had to "fight the good fight of faith."

Then I thought of the little church in which they found their fellowship. It was besieged by continual assaults of their Jewish foes. It was torn with internal divisions. It was honeycombed by deadly heresies. It was defiled by sensuality. Nearly all the members of the church were of obscure origin and standing. Many of them were slaves. It was in these conditions of fierce and growing difficulties that these disciples had to be good soldiers of Jesus Christ. And it is to this little company of Christian recruits that the apostle sends this challenging letter in which is found the rousing bugle-peal of my text. "Watch ye, stand fast in the faith, quit you like men, be strong."

Now I will confess to you that times and again during the last few months this trumpet-blast has sounded in my ears, as though it were a clarion-call to the Christians of to-day. For we too have our warfare upon a most exacting field. We have fallen upon gravely troubled times. We are witnessing a resurgence of devilry that is perfectly appalling. The baser passions have become frightfully aggressive, and a crude animalism is at large like a surging, boiling sea which has burst its dykes. Some of us had begun to dream that the sweet angel of peace was almost at our gates, and that nothing could happen to drive her away; and now, when we look out of the gate, it is no fair angel-messenger which we see, but the red fury of unprecedented strife and slaughter. And amid all this we have to live the Christian life.

But it is not only the "fightings without" which trouble us. There are also "the fears within." Many of our venerable assumptions are lying in ruin. Our spiritual world has suffered an upheaval as though with the convulsion of an earthquake, and many of us are trembling and confused. What then shall we do in this terrible hour? What path shall we take? Can we settle our goings upon any promising road of purpose and endeavour? Along what lines shall we pull ourselves together? And in answer to all these questions I bring you this well-tried counsel of the great Christian apostle, this bugle-peal from the first century, and I ask you to let it be to you as the inspired word of the living God. "Watch ye, stand fast in the faith, quit you like men, be strong." Let us examine the counsel in order that we may buckle it on to our souls.

Here then is the first note of this soldierly blast. "Watch ye!" The phrase literally means "keep awake!" You perhaps think there is no need of that counsel to-day. You probably think that in times like these our difficulty is not to keep awake but to go to sleep. I am not so sure about that. If we have loved ones at the war there will not be the remotest peril of our going to sleep. Every post that comes to our door will startle us like the crack of doom. Every headline in the daily press will tighten our nerves in sleepless attention. But when we have no flesh and blood at the front, when many miles roll between us and the fields of war, when we are only spectators, a certain drowsiness is not so far away as we may suppose. When we only read about things, things become familiar, and the familiar is apt to lose its terror. Custom is a dull narcotic, and frequent repetition dims our apprehension. When the Titanic went down the whole city spoke in whispers, such a dread was resting over our souls. But now a dreadnought goes down, or a half dozen cruisers, and we scarcely catch our breath at the news. The cushion of familiarity is thickening between us and realities, and awful facts do not hit us on the raw. The awful becomes less awful by repetition, and we grow less sensitive as the tragedies increase. The newspaper statistics cease to be significant, and the descriptive adjectives become the tamest blanks. And therefore there is need for the apostle's trumpet blast to sound in our ears. "Keep awake!" Do not let familiarity become an opiate, so putting the senses to sleep that the direst woes become a painless commonplace. "Keep awake!" Make it a matter of will. Bring the stream of vital thought to bear upon the field. Exercise the imagination. Nourish the sympathies. We must keep awake, for our primary hope of emancipation in this dark hour is to remain sensitive, to be capable of being shocked and wounded with the appalling blows of every succeeding day.

But it is not only wakefulness, but also watchfulness which the apostle enjoins in the counsel of our text. The soldier of Jesus is to be awake and watchful with all the keen quest of a sentinel peering about him night and day. But our watchfulness must be intelligent and disciplined, and we must carefully survey the entire field. We must keep awake, and we must diligently watch for all enemies of the sanctified brotherhood of the race, as a sentry would watch every suspicious movement in the night. What are the real enemies behind all the appalling desolation and sorrow of our time? Is it militarism? Then "Watch ye!" Is it something deeper than militarism? Is it racial animosity and jealousy and prejudice? Then "Watch ye!" Is it something even deeper than racial antipathy? Is it a profound and deadly materialism in all the nations—a materialism which has been tricked out in the ribbons of culture, and disguised in the glamour of progress? Then "Keep awake, Watch ye!" Or is it a faithless church, muttering many shibboleths, but confessing no vital faith; a church which has been too much a pretense, offering no strong moral and spiritual preservatives, and supplying no saving salt to social fellowships, and, therefore, not exercising any restraint upon moral degeneracy and corruption? "Keep awake, and Watch ye!"

And amid all the horrors and agonies of our day fasten your eyes upon the real enemy of the Lord Jesus, the outstanding antagonist of His kingdom of righteousness and truth.

But there is a further word to say about our vigilance. We must keep awake and watchful, not only to detect the busy lurking, ambushed foes, but also to see all the bright and wonderful things of the hour, all the splendid happenings which are favourable to the holy will and Kingdom of our Lord. What should we think of a sentinel who could not distinguish between enemy and friend? And what shall we say of a soldier-sentinel of Christ who has no eye for the great and friendly happenings on the field? Watch ye, and behold the growing seriousness of the world; frivolity has almost begun to apologize for itself, and tinselled gaiety is ill at ease. Watch ye, and behold the unsealing of multitudinous springs of human sympathy, and the flowing of holy currents from the ends of the earth. Watch ye, and behold the magnificent courage which in every land of strife is purging families from the dross of indolence and indifference, and educing the gold of chivalry and sacrifice. Watch ye, and behold the marvellous re-equipment of Christian motive—thousands upon thousands of Christian disciples realizing as they have never done before that the world needs the vital redeeming grace of the Lord Jesus, and that without Him human brotherhood will remain a phantom and a dream. A real wakeful watchman will see these things. He will not only record the things of the night and the nightmares, but he will be as "they who watch for the morning." The Moslem priest appears on the tower of his mosque half an hour after sunset to call the people to prayer, but he also appears on the tower half an hour before sunrise, when the grey gleams of morning are faintly falling upon the night. And we too, watchmen of Jesus, must watch for the sunrise as well as for the sunsets, and we too must tell what fair jewels of hope we see shining on the dark robe of the night. Brethren, the Lord Jesus Christ is abroad! "Watch ye, for at such an hour as ye think not, the Son of Man will come."

Now let us consider the second note of the counsel which is given by this warrior, Paul. "Stand fast in the faith." Just try to realize that bracing counsel coming to these young recruits in the city of Corinth. Let me try to paraphrase it as I think it would be interpreted to them. "When the soft, enervating air of Corinth's luxuriousness steals over you like the mild air of Lotus-Land, 'Stand fast in the faith'! When the cold wind of persecution assails you like an icy blast from the north, 'Stand fast in the faith'! If some supercilious philosopher comes along and breathes cynically upon your new-found piety and devotion, 'Stand fast in the faith'! Stand fast in your faith and meet all your antagonisms there."

And has that counsel no pertinency for the Christian believers of our own time? There are some among us who are ready, because of the unspeakable horrors through which we are passing, to throw their faith away like obsolete arms and armour. Now men who can drop their faith in the day of real emergency have never been really held by it. That is surely true; men who can drop their faith like a handkerchief have never known their faith as a strong and vital defence. And yet that is what you sometimes find them doing in modern novels. They just drop their faith as they would drop a pair of gloves. Robert Elsmere, in Mrs. Humphry Ward's story of twenty years ago, dropped his faith in about ten days. If my memory serves me truly, George Eliot dropped her faith in about the same length of time. If our faith has ever meant anything vital, it will be as difficult to drop it as to drop our skin. But it is the inexperienced who are in peril. It is the young recruit who is dangerously convulsed by the upheavals of our day, and it is to him I bring the nerving counsel of the Lord: "Stand fast in the faith!"

"Stand fast in the faith!" What faith? "The faith once for all delivered to the saints." Stand fast in the faith of the atoning Saviour as the secret of the reconciliation of mankind. Stand fast in the faith of the risen Lord as the secret and promise of racial union and brotherhood. Stand fast in the faith of the Holy Spirit as the source of all the light and cheer which illumines the race. Stand fast in your own personal faith in the exalted Lord. Don't doubt Him! Don't suspect Him! Don't desert Him! Above all, don't sell Him! In this hour of darkness, when devilry seems to be pulling down the very pillars of the temple, stand fast in the faith, and let this be your strong but humble cry:

"Although the fig-tree shall not blossom,
Neither shall fruit be in the vines;
The labour of the olive shall fail,
And the fields shall yield no meat;
The flock shall be cut off from the fold,
And there shall be no herd in the stalls:
Yet I will rejoice in the Lord,
I will joy in the God of my salvation."

 And the third note in the great apostle's counsel in this: "Quit you like men." Our translators have taken four words to express a single word in the original letter. We have no one English word which can carry the splendid load of meaning. It really means—play the man! It really means—no funk! All the school children will know the value of that word. It is a good strong vital English word, and I am sure it expresses the spirit of the apostle's counsel to these young recruits. Lowell uses it in the Bigelow Papers: "To funk right out o' p'litical strife ain't thought to be the thing." No funk, soldiers of Christ! I have sometimes heard men talk of late as though the Lord were dead, and the game is up, and the Kingdom is in ruins. "Play the man!" The European soldiers of every nation are showing the world in their own sphere what it means to play the man. Some of us are becoming almost afraid to call ourselves soldiers of Jesus when we see what a true soldier really is. Think of it! Think of his readiness for the front! Think of his laughter in sacrifice! Think of his song in the midst of danger and pain! Think of his endurance even unto death! And then, think how we stand up and sing "Onward, Christian soldiers, marching as to war"! And shall we funk in the day of darkness and disaster, and after months of appalling bloodshed and woe shall we talk as if the campaign of righteousness were ended, and the Kingdom of Jesus is overturned? Let us stop this kind of talk. Let us silence this sort of fear. Let us crush this type of disloyalty. It is an insult to our flag; it is a dishonour to our Lord.

"Quit you like men, be strong!" Put strength into everything, and do everything strongly. Do not let us speak or serve in a faint, lax, irresolute, anæmic, dying sort of way. "Be strong!" Be strong in your prayers. Be strong in your moral and spiritual ambitions. Be strong in your visions and hopes. Be strong in your beneficence; strengthen it to the vigour of sacrifice. And if there be a devil, as more than ever I believe there is, let the Church surprise him by her strength. Let her turn the day of calamity into the day of opportunity. Let her transfigure the hour of disaster into the hour of deeper consecration. Let us make new vows. Let us enter into new devotion. Let us exercise ourselves in new chivalry. Let us go out in new ways of sacrifice. My brethren, God is not dead! "Watch ye, stand fast in the faith, quit you like men, be strong!"

"Stand up, stand up for Jesus!
The trumpet call obey;
Forth to the mighty conflict
In this His glorious day.
Ye that are men now serve Him
Against unnumbered foes,
Let courage rise with danger
And strength to strength oppose.

"Stand up, stand up for Jesus!
Ye soldiers of the Cross.
Lift high His royal banner,
It must not suffer loss.
From victory unto victory
His army shall He lead,
Till every foe is vanquished,
And Christ is Lord indeed!"

X: ENDURING HARDNESS

Heavenly Father, may all our hearts be filled with Thy praise. May the spirit of Thanksgiving fill all our days, and deliver us from the mood of murmuring and complaint. Graciously remove the scales from our eyes, so that we may look upon our life with eyes anointed with the eye-salve of grace. Help us to discern Thy footprints in the ordinary road. Grant that we may now review our yesterdays and see the providences which have crowded our paths. Help us to see Thy name on blessings that we never recognized, so that we may now be praiseful where we have been indifferent. Redeem us from our spiritual sloth. Awake us out of our perilous sleep. May our consciences goad us when we are in peril. May the good desires within us be so strengthened as to destroy every desire that is vain. Sow in our hearts the word of Thy truth. Guard the seed with the vigilance of Thy blessed Spirit, and let it appear in our life as a fragrant and bountiful harvest. Graciously watch us and defend us and make us mighty in consecration, and may we place our all upon the altar. Amen.

"Thou therefore endure hardness as a good soldier of Jesus Christ." 2 Timothy 2:3.

Any military metaphor which is used to-day will surely have a very arresting significance. Many of our hymns are crowded with military terminology. In the Wesleyan Methodist Hymn-Book there is a whole section entitled "For Believers Fighting." We are all familiar with these martial hymns: "Onward, Christian Soldiers", "The Son of God goes forth to war", "Soldiers of Christ arise", "Stand up, stand up, for Jesus, ye soldiers of the cross", "Oft in danger, oft in woe, onward Christians, onward go." But too often the soldier-like hymn is only a bit of martial poetry which pleases the emotions but does not stir the will. We like the swing of the theme. It brings a sort of exhilaration into our moods, just as lively dance music awakes a nimble restlessness in our feet. Too often it is the song of the parade ground, and it is not broken with the awful thundering of the guns in actual war. But just now when we hear the phrase, "Endure hardness as a good soldier," our thoughts are carried away to the battlefields of Europe. We recall those roads like deeply ploughed fields! Those fields scooped by the shells into graves in which you can bury a score of men! Those trenches filling with the rain or snows, the hiding place of disease, and assailed continually with the most frightful engines of destruction! Pestilence on the prowl! Frost stiffening the limbs into benumbment! Death always possible before the next breath! These military metaphors in our hymns get some red blood into them when we use them against backgrounds and scenes like these. "Endure hardness as a good soldier."

Now the apostle calls for this soldierly spirit in Thessalonica. He is writing to young recruits in the army of the Lord. They are having their first baptism of fire. Their enemies are strong, subtle, ubiquitous. To be a Christian in Thessalonica was to face the fierce onslaught of overwhelming odds. But indeed in those early days, Christian believers, wherever they lived, had to be heroic in the defence of their faith and obedience. Everywhere circumstances were hostile. Nothing was won without sacrifice. Nothing was held without blood. To be a witness was to be a martyr. If a believer would be faithful to his Lord he must "fight the good fight of faith"; if he would extend the frontiers of the Kingdom of Heaven he must endure hardness as a good soldier of Jesus Christ.

What are the circumstances amid which the modern Church is placed? The Christian believer in our day is confronted with stupendous difficulties. Look at the present field on which our Christian warfare is to be waged. When the European war broke out I was staying at a quiet seaside village, from which I could see the soft green beauty of the mountains which encircle the English lakes. On the morning that war was proclaimed I felt as though some venerable and majestic temple had suddenly crumbled into dust. One of my most intimate friends, a noble German, was staying in my home, and we both felt as though some devil of mischief and disaster had toppled human affairs into confusion. The quiet sequence of human progress seemed to have been smashed at a stroke. The nations drew apart, and gulfs of isolation yawned between them, and down the gulfs there swept the cruel shrieking blasts of racial hatred and antipathy. Holy ministries which had been leagued in sacred fellowship were wrenched asunder. Spiritual communions which had been sweet and welcome curdled in the biting blast of resentment. The work of the Kingdom of our Lord was smitten as by an enemy; ploughshares were beaten into swords; pruning-hooks were transformed into spears; and instead of the fir and the myrtle-tree there sprang up the thorns and the briars. And then, to crown our difficulties, the red fury of war leaped into countries where our missionaries are proclaiming the gospel of peace, and the passion of battle began to burn where they are telling the story of the passion of Calvary, that holy passion of sacrifice which brought to the whole world redemption from sin, and reconciliation with God, and the promise of the life that now is, and of that which is to come.

Our immediate circumstances do not offer the soldiers of Jesus an easy parade ground where we can just loll and sing our lilting songs; they rather offer us a fearfully rugged and broken field which demands as heroic and chivalrous virtues as ever clothed a child of God. What shall we do? Is it the hour for craven fear or for a noble courage? What shall we do on our mission fields? Shall we cry "forward," or shall we sound the depressing and despairing note of retreat? Shall we throw up the sponge, or shall we, in the spirit of unprecedented sacrifice, march forward in our campaign, and endure hardness as good soldiers of Jesus Christ?

First of all, we must keep our eyes steadily fixed upon the object for which Christ died, that solemn and holy end for which He created and appointed His own Church. And what is that object? It is to let "all men know that all men move under a canopy of love" as broad as the blue sky above. It is to break down all middle walls of partition, and to merge the sundered peoples in the quickening communion of His grace. It is to unite all the kingdoms of the world in the one and radiant Kingdom of His love. That is the aim and purpose of our blessed Lord, and in all the shock and convulsions of to-day we must keep that object steadfastly in sight. It was said of Napoleon that "he never for a moment lost sight of his way onward in the dazzle and uproar of present circumstances." That is to say, Napoleon was never blinded by the glare of victory or by the lowering cloud of defeat. "He saw only the object." Quietness did not throw its perilous spell about him. Calamity did not turn his eyes from the forward way. He saw only the object, and the glory of the goal sent streams of energy into his will and into his feet at every step of the changing road.

Now our temptation is to permit events to determine our sight. There is the shimmer of gold on the right hand, and we turn to covet. There is the gleam of the sword on the left hand, and we turn in fear. We allow circumstances to govern our aims. Our eyes are deflected from their object by the dazzle or the uproar around us. And here is the peril of it all. When we lose the object of our warfare we begin to lose the campaign. And, therefore, one of the first necessities of the Christian Church in the present hour is to have our Lord's own purpose steadily in view, to keep her eyes glued upon that supreme end, and to allow nothing to turn her aside. "Let thine eyes look right on;" "Thy kingdom come;" "The kingdoms of this world shall become the Kingdom of our God;" "He must reign until He hath put all enemies under His feet." This, I say, is the pressing and immediate need of the good soldier of Christ Jesus, to refuse to have his single aim complicated by the entanglement of passing circumstances, and to constantly "apprehend that for which we also were apprehended by Christ Jesus our Lord."

What else shall we do in this hour of upheaval and disaster? The Church must eclipse the exploits of carnal warfare by the more glorious warfare of the spirit. Just recall the heroisms which are happening every day in Europe, and on which the eyes of the world are riveted with an almost mesmerized wonder! Think of the magnificent sacrifices! Think of the splendid courage! Think of the exquisite chivalry! Think of the incredible powers of endurance! And then, further, think that the Church of Christ is called upon to outshine these glories with demonstrations more glorious still.

This was surely one of the outstanding distinctions of apostolic life. Whenever hostilities confronted the early Church, whenever the first disciples were opposed by the gathered forces of the world, wherever the sword was bared and active, wherever tyranny exulted in sheer brutality, these early disciples unveiled a more splendid strength, and threw the carnal power into the shade. They faced their difficulties with such force and splendour of character that their very antagonisms became only the dark background on which the glory of the Lord was more manifestly revealed. Their courage rose with danger and eclipsed it!

Let me open one or two windows in the apostolic record which give us glimpses of this conquering life. Here, then, is a glimpse of the hostilities: "Let us straightly threaten them that they speak henceforth to no man in this name." There you have the naked tyranny of carnal power, and there you have the threat that burns through carnal speech. And now, over against that power put the action of the Church: "And they spake the word of God with boldness!" They were good soldiers of Jesus Christ, and by that boldness the tyranny and threat of carnal power were completely eclipsed.

Here is another glimpse of those heroic days: "And when they had called the apostles, and beaten them, they commanded that they should not speak in the name of Jesus." There again you have the demonstration of carnal power; and here again is the demonstration of the power of the spirit: "And they departed from the presence of the counsel, rejoicing that they were counted worthy to suffer shame for his name. And they ceased not to teach and preach Jesus Christ." I say that this "rejoicing" eclipses that beating, and the good soldier of Jesus Christ puts the Roman soldier into the shade.

Let me open another window: "And they cast Stephen out of the city and stoned him." Get your eyes on that display of carnal passion and tyranny; and then lift your eyes upon the victim of it: "And he kneeled down and cried with a loud voice, Lord, lay not this sin to their charge." Who is the conqueror in that tragedy, the stoners or the stoned, the ministers of destruction or the good soldier of Jesus Christ? The carnal power was terrific and deadly, but it was utterly eclipsed by the power of grace, the power which blazed forth in this redeemed and consecrated life. Open yet another window upon this day of shining exploits: "Having stoned Paul they drew him out of the city, supposing he had been dead." That incident seems to record the coronation and sovereignty of brutal strength. Now read: "And they returned again to Lystra." Paul went back to the place where he had been stoned, to tell again the good news of grace, and to carry to broken people the ministries of healing. And I say that this bruised man, beaten and sore, returning again to the scene of the stoning, is a good soldier of Jesus Christ, and by his magnificent courage and grace he eclipsed all the rough strength of the world and threw its achievements into the shade.

But it is not only in apostolic days that you can find these brilliant contrasts. The Church has been distinguished by such demonstrations of spiritual glory all along her history. When material power has been riotous and rampant, when rude, crude passions have blazed through the earth, the chivalry of the Church has shone resplendent in the murky night, and she has eclipsed the dread shocks of the world and the flesh and the devil by her noble sacrifices, and by her serenity, and by her spontaneous joy. The Church has distinguished herself by her manifestations of spiritual strength, by her lofty Christian purpose, by her glowing devotional enthusiasm, and this over against gigantic obstacles, and in the face of enemies who seemed to be overwhelming.

I think of James Chalmers, the martyred missionary of New Guinea. How well I remember the last time I met him; his big, powerful body, his lion-like head, his shock of rough hair, his face with such a strange commingling of strength and gentleness, indomitableness and grace! And what he went through in New Guinea in carrying to the natives the story of our Saviour's love! And then, having gone through it all, he stood up there in England, on the platform of Exeter Hall, and said: "Recall these twenty-one years, give me back all its experiences, give me its shipwrecks, give me its standings in the face of death, give it me surrounded with savages with spears and clubs, give it me back again with spears flying about me, with the club knocking me to the ground, give it me back, and I will still be your missionary." What is happening in Europe just now that can put that exploit in the shade? I do not wonder that when that man thought of heaven he used these words: "There will be much visiting in heaven, and much work. I guess I shall have good mission work to do, great, brave work for Christ. He will have to find it, for I can be nothing else than a missionary." James Chalmers went back to New Guinea to tell and retell to the natives why Jesus came to thee and me and all men, and he won the martyr's crown. The love of Christ constrained him. And again I ask, what incidents in carnal warfare are not eclipsed by shining heroisms like these?

I might go on telling you these glorious exploits of grace, but I hasten to say that it is our privilege to continue the story. To-day carnal strength is stalking in deadly stride through a whole continent. And to-day the Church must do something so splendid and so heroic as will outshine the glamour of material war. This is the hour when we must send out more men and women who are willing to live and toil and die for the Hindu, and for the Turk, and the Persian, and the Chinese and the Japanese, and all the dusky sons of Africa. I verily believe that if the apostle Paul were in our midst to-day, with the war raging in Europe, he would sound an advance all along the line. He would call us in this hour to send out more men and women to save, and to comfort, and to heal; men and women who will lay down their lives in bringing life to their fellow-men. We must send forth new army corps of the soldiers of Christ, and we must give them more abundant means, endowing them so plentifully that they can go out into the needy places of Asia and Africa, and assuage the pains and burdens of the body, and dispel the darkness of the mind, and give liberty to the imprisoned spirit, and lead the souls of men into the life and joy and peace of our blessed Lord. If the Church would, and if the Church will, she can so arrest the attention and win the hearts of the natives of Africa and Asia with the grace and gentleness of the Lord Jesus, a grace and gentleness made incarnate again in you and me, and in those whom we send to the field, that the excellent glory of the Spirit shall shine pre-eminent, and in this hour of world-wide disaster the risen Lord shall again be glorified.

Shall we quietly challenge ourselves amid all the awful happenings of to-day? Here are the terms of the challenge. Shall the good soldier of Christ Jesus be overshadowed by the soldiers of the world? Or shall the courage and ingenuities of the world be eclipsed by the heroism and the wise audacity of the Church? Shall we withdraw our army from the field because the war is raging in Europe, or shall we send it reinforcements? Shall we practice a more severe economy and straiten our army's equipment for service; or shall we practice a more glorious self-sacrifice, and make its equipment more efficient? Shall we exalt and glorify our Saviour, or shall we allow Him to be put in the shade? Shall we endure hardness, as good soldiers of Christ, or shall we take to the fields of indulgence, and allow the Church of the Living God to be outshone by the army of the world? Which shall it be?

Our holy battlefield is as wide as the world. The needs are clamant. The opportunities of victory are on every side. Our Captain is calling! What then, shall it be? Advance or retreat? What answer can there be but one? Surely the answer must be that we will advance, even though it mean the shedding of the blood of sacrifice.

One of our medical missionaries was Dr. Francis J. Hall of Peking, China. He had been graduated with high honours at the Johns Hopkins Medical School in Baltimore, and had consecrated his life to medical missionary work in China, where his large abilities promptly won him wide influence. In 1913 he said to one of his associates: "I have just been called to a Chinese who has typhus fever. Many physicians have died of that disease, but I must go." Two weeks later he was stricken. As he lay dying his mind wandered, and he was heard to exclaim: "I hear them calling, I must go; I hear them calling!" Do we hear them calling? Is the answer "Yes"? Then let us joyfully register a vow that, God helping us, the army of the Lord shall not be maimed because of our indifference, but as good soldiers of Jesus Christ we will, if need be, endure hardness, and give of our possessions, even unto the shedding of our blood.

XI: THE INVISIBLE COMMANDER

Eternal God, we rejoice in the security that is offered to us in our midnights and in our noons. Thou wilt not leave us to the loneliness of self-communion, but Thou wilt hold fellowship with us along the way. Come to us as the Lord Jesus came to the men who were journeying to Emmaus, and make our hearts burn within us in the revelation of light and grace. Especially in these bewildering times wilt Thou steady our minds with Thy councils and inspire our hearts in the assurance of Thy sovereign love. Lead us along our troubled road. Let the heavenly light break upon our darkness. Help us to believe in Thy peace even when the world is at strife. Let Thy kingdom come. Even when the world is filled with the smoke of battle may we discern the presence of the Lord. Save us from the sin of unbelief. Reveal to us, we humbly pray Thee, the sin in which this strife has been born, and help the nations to turn from it in new consecration to Thee. In this gracious purpose wilt Thou possess our services. Help us to look beyond the seen into the strength and glory of the unseen. Cheer us with Thy consolations. Uphold us with Thine hand, and impart to us the gift of Thy gracious peace. Amen.

"And He will lift up an ensign to the nations from far, and will hiss unto them from the end of the earth." Isaiah 5:26.

"And it shall come to pass in that day that the Lord shall hiss for the fly that is in the uttermost part of the rivers of Egypt, and for the bee that is in the land of Assyria." Isaiah 7:18.

That was a startling word to fall upon the ears of the people of Judah. It shocked them into confusion. It was an altogether revolutionary word. It played havoc with their traditional beliefs. It smashed up all their easy securities. It turned their world upside down, and all their ancient confidences were broken. Let us try to feel the shock of the message. The people had come to regard their land as a sort of divine reservation, and they looked upon their nation as a specially favoured instrument in the hand of the Lord. They esteemed themselves as being in the friendly grip and fellowship of the Lord of hosts. All their movements were the inspirations of His counsels, and in the strength of His providence their nation's progress and destiny were assured. They lived in the assumption that every step in their national life was foreseen, and planned, and provided for, and that they were always being led towards divinely appointed goals. There was nothing of chance in their journeyings, and nothing of uncertainty in their ends. For them there was no blind groping in the darkness, for the Lord of hosts had charge of their national life; and "the sure mercies of David" would secure it from calamity and destruction.

That was what they thought about themselves. What did they think of the nations beyond their frontier? That was quite another story. They looked upon other nations as struggling blindly, and in their dark rage imagining vain things. These other nations had the promptings of passion, but they had no divine and mystic leadership. They moved hither and thither, but it was under no divine appointment, and a thousand traps were laid for their unhallowed feet. Yonder was Assyria, full of strength and full of movement, expressing herself in the might of tremendous armies, but she was under no divine command or inspiration. Assyria was like a boat in unknown waters, without a pilot, and she was marked for inevitable destruction. And yonder was proud Egypt, swelling with her power and renown, colossal in her material achievements, but she had no divinely enlightened eyes, she was blind in her goings, and her marching was in reality a staggering towards doom. And yonder were other nations from afar; but they were all just chance masses, looked upon as existing outside the frontier line of divine favour and enlightenment. They dwelt in some hinterland of life where God's gracious decrees do not run. They were beyond the orbit of divine thought and grace. Now that was the kind of thinking which the prophet had to meet. Judah regarded herself as nestling within the home circle of Providence, and all other nations were outcasts living beyond the sacred pale.

And now perhaps we shall be able to feel something of the astounding effect of the prophet's words. "And the Lord shall lift up an ensign to the nations from far." Far-away peoples are to move under the impulse and inspiration of the Lord, and in the light of His guiding command. "The Lord shall hiss for the fly that is in the uttermost part of the rivers of Egypt." A far-away nation, thick as flies, is to move under the touch and ordination of God! "The Lord shall hiss for the bee that is in the land of Assyria." A far-away nation, thick as a hive of bees, is to move under the controlling purpose of the Lord! Can you feel the shock of the prophet's words? It is the shock of a larger thought which shakes the nations out of their small and cosey contentment. They had conceived the divine Providence as being confined exclusively to Judah's particular guidance and defence. They had thought within the limits of a country; they are now bidden to cross the frontier and conceive a Providence which encircles a continent and a world. The fly in Egypt, and the bee in Assyria, raising their wings at the touch of the Lord,—it staggered them into incredulity!

Now we can see what the prophet was doing. He was seeking to enlarge their sense of the orbit of the divine movement. For the little ripples on their pool he was substituting the ocean tides. For the circle of their native hills and valleys he was substituting a line which embraced the uttermost parts of the earth. And that is what I wish to do in this meditation. I wish to proclaim the vastness of the divine orbit, the tremendous sweep of the divine decrees, and I wish to emphasize the teaching of this great prophet, that momentous destinies may be born in far-away places, even at the very end of the world. "The Lord shall hiss for the fly that is in the uttermost part of the rivers of Egypt, and for the bee that is in the land of Assyria."

Well then, under the power of this teaching, let us think in wider orbits of the divine inspiration of nations. For we are apt to imprison our thought within very narrow and artificial restraints. Much of our thought about providential movements shuts God up to the circle of so-called Christian nations: But what if a fierce and decadent civilization is to be corrected by the inspired influence of such peoples as are described by Rudyard Kipling as "lesser breeds without the law?" What if our God will hiss for the fly and the bee among just such peoples as we are inclined to patronize or despise? Let us imagine some modern Isaiah standing up in London or New York and uttering words like these;—"The Lord shall hiss for the fly that is in the uttermost part of China, and for the bee that is in the land of India." I know that such a doctrine shocks our national susceptibilities, just as a similar doctrine shocked the national pride of the ancient Jews. But such a doctrine offers the only true interpretation of the range of the divine orbit. It may be that the reinforcements of civilization are to come from the movements of the stagnant waters of China. It may be that rivers of vitality are to flow into our life from the meditative, contemplative, philosophic, mystic races of India. Just think of their quiet, lofty, serious brooding, stealing into our feverish materialism and sobering the fierceness of the quest. I cannot but wonder what the good Lord, in the vastness of His orbit, is even now preparing for the world on the far-away plains of India and China.

Let your imagination exercise itself again in the larger orbit, and think of some modern prophet standing up in London with this message upon his lips;—"The Lord shall hiss for the fly that is in the uttermost parts of Russia." The message strikes us as incredible, but it is only because, like the people of Judah, our conception of the divine orbit is so small and circumscribed. I for one am watching with fascinated eyes the movements of Russia. I am wondering what is coming to us from that great people, so long and patiently sad, so full of reverence, going on long, weary pilgrimages to bow at holy shrines. Superstition? Yes, if you please. But I am wondering what is going to happen when the dogged strength of that superstition becomes an enlightened faith. I am wondering what will happen when that rich, fertile bed of national reverence begins to bear the full and matured fruits of the Spirit. What then? I know it is not easy to think it. It is not easy to widen the orbit of one's thought. It is never easy to stretch a neglected or unused muscle. But the wider thought is the orbit of our God, and in the mysterious land of Russia untold destinies may be even now at the birth.

And so do I urge that we think in vaster orbits of the divine inspiration of nations. Let us reject the atheism of incredulity, and let us encourage ourselves in the boundless hope of an all-encompassing God of the human race. The great God journeys on in His tremendous orbit, and who knows from what unlikely peoples the rejuvenation of the world is to come? "The Lord shall hiss for the fly that is in the uttermost part of the rivers of Egypt, and for the bee that is in the land of Assyria."

Now I want to go further, and under the power of the prophet's teaching I would urge that we think in wide orbits of the divine raising of the heroic leaders of men. In what wide and mysterious sweeps the great God works when He wants a leader of men! The man is wanted here at the center, but he is being prepared yonder on the remote circumference! God hisses for the fly or the bee, and He calls it from very obscure and unlikely fields.

Here is ancient Israel. Her altars are defiled, and her balances are perverted. She is hollow in worship, and she is crooked in trade, and the people are listless in their debasement. A leader is wanted to awake and scourge the people. Where shall he be found? The Lord hisses for a fly in Tekoa, a wretched little village, in a mean and scanty setting; and the fly was a poor herdman, following the flock, and eking out his miserable living by gathering the figs of the sycamore. And this Amos was God's man! A prophet of fire was wanted in Bethel, and God prepared him in Tekoa! But what an orbit, and who would have thought that Tekoa would have been a school of the prophets?

Stride across the centuries. The religion of Europe has become a gloss for indulgence. Nay, it has become an excuse for it. The Father's house has become a den of thieves. The doctrines of grace have been wiped out by a system of man-devised works. Religion is devitalized, and morals have become dissolute. Wanted, a man, who shall be both scourge and evangelist! Where shall he be found? "The Lord hissed for the fly" that was in Eisleben, in the house of a poor miner, and Martin Luther came forth to grapple with all the corruptions of established religion. But what an orbit! A fire was wanted to burn up the refuse which had accumulated over spiritual religion, and the fire was first kindled in a little home, in a little village, far away from the broad highways of social privilege and advantage. Again, I say, what an orbit!

March forward again across the years. Here is England under the oppression of a king who claims divine sanction for his oppression. There is no tyranny like the tyranny which stamps itself with a holy seal. And in those old days of Charles I, tyranny wore a sacred badge. Tyranny carried a cross. It was tyranny by divine right. Wrong was justified by grace. I say, of all tyrannies, this is the most tyrannical. Wanted, a man to meet and overthrow it! Where will he be found? Will he be found in some national centre of learning where wealthy privilege holds her seat? Oh, no! The Lord hissed for a fly on the fens, from a little farm at Huntington, and Oliver Cromwell emerged, to try swords with the king on his throne! Let me give the familiar glimpse which Sir Philip Warwick offers us of Cromwell making his first speech in the House of Commons. "I came into the House one morning, well clad, and perceived a gentleman speaking whom I knew not, very ordinarily apparelled, for it was a plain cloth suit, which seemed to have been made by an ill country tailor. His linen was plain and not very clean, and I remember a speck or two of blood upon his little band, which was not much larger than his collar. His hat was without a hat-band. His stature was of a good size; his sword stuck close to his side; his countenance swollen and reddish; his voice sharp and untunable, and his eloquence full of fervour." And there is God's man! But what an orbit! A man was wanted for the defence of liberty and spiritual religion, and God prepared this man in the obscurity of a little farm among the fens. What an orbit is marked by the goings of the Lord. The Lord hissed for the fly on the fen.

March forward across the centuries. Here is slavery in the American republic. In spite of the noble words of the Declaration of Independence: "That all men are created equal; that they are endowed by their Creator with certain inalienable rights; that among these are life, liberty and the pursuit of happiness"—in spite of these ringing human claims slavery nestled beneath the American flag. Well, wanted a man to deal with it! Where will he be found? Will he be found in some university centre? Will he be a paragon of intellectual learning and accomplishment? Oh no! The Lord hissed for a fly in Harden, in a scraggy part of Kentucky, Harden with its "barren hillocks and weedy hollows, and stunted and scrubby underbush,"—and there in a dismal solitude, and in a cheerless home, and in the deepest poverty, the great God made His man, and Abraham Lincoln came forth to cross swords with the great wrong, and to ring the bells of freedom from the "frozen North to the glowing South, and from the stormy waters of the Atlantic westward to the calmer waters of the Pacific Main." But what an orbit of divine providence! Who would have guessed that just there, in that poor, unschooled, and unprivileged family the great God was doing His momentous work? And I wonder where now in the vast orbit of His providence He is rearing the leaders of to-morrow? Our God moves in mighty sweeps, and He is even now at work in the mysterious ministries of His grace. "The Lord shall hiss for the fly that is in the uttermost part of the rivers of Egypt and for the bee that is in the land of Assyria."

And then, under the influence of the prophet's teaching I want once more to urge that we think in wider orbits of the divine presence in the individual life. For instance, in what sweeping orbits the Lord moves on His journeys in seeking to bring us to Himself, and to fashion us into the strength and beauty of His own image. He lifts an ensign to some remote circumstance, and from afar there comes an influence which sets me on the road to God. He calls a ministry from distant Egypt, or from far off Assyria, and my life is turned to the home of my Lord.

Here is a careless young son of wealth in Cambridge University. Life for him is just an idle sport, a careless revel, a jaunty outing, an enjoyable extravagance. Life is just a shallow, shimmering pool; not an ocean with momentous tidal forces, and with the voice of the great Eternal speaking in its mighty tones. Wanted a man to awake this indolent son of wealth! And in what an orbit God moved to find the man! The Lord hissed for a fly in Massachusetts, and there, in Northfield, was a poor homestead, encumbered with mortgage; and a poor widow with seven children, so poor that the very kindling wood was taken by the creditors from the shed. And there in that poor woman's house God made His man, and Dwight Moody came forth, and went to Cambridge University, and proclaimed the evangel of grace, and by the love of God won this young fellow from a loose and jaunty and indifferent life, and kindled in him a passionate devotion to Christ which is now blazing away on the Southern Soudan in a campaign to light a line of Christian beacon-fires which shall stretch from coast to coast! But what an orbit! From a poor widow's homestead in Northfield to a sporting young fellow in Cambridge University!

I met a cultured man the other day, a man who has enjoyed all the academic advantages that money can provide, a man of university culture and distinction, but whose life has been spiritually indifferent, and who has held coldly aloof from God and the Kingdom of God. And in the vast orbit of His providence the great God brought this man into communion with Billy Sunday, and all the stubble of his neglected life was burned up in the consuming fire of his kindled love for the Lord. But just think of the orbit! The Lord hissed for His fly, and from the apparently incredible circumstance of a slangy evangelist this man was brought to his Father's House in reconciliation and peace. Again I say, what an orbit! "I will bring the blind by a way that they know not," and under His wide and mysterious leadership the blind find themselves at home.

And so, my friends, our God is still moving in these vast orbits. He hisses for a disappointment, and it comes and throws its shadow upon our life, but the shadow is purposed to be one of the healing shadows of grace. "I will command the clouds, saith the Lord." Yes, even our cloudy experiences move under command. They travel in the tremendous orbit of His providence. "I will command the ravens, saith the Lord God." Yes, there are diverse circumstances that come to us on wings,—kind words, cheering messages, bright inspirations, and they are the commanded ministers of God's providence. They are God's messengers on wings!

We can never tell in what remote circumstances the good Lord is even now preparing our to-morrow. But of one thing we may be perfectly sure, the great Lord is at work, and He is at work over wide fields. "Rest in the Lord, and wait patiently for Him." "The Lord is thy keeper.... The Lord shall keep thee from all evil, He shall keep thy soul. The Lord shall keep thy going out and thy coming in from this time forth, and even for evermore."

XII: THE SOLDIER'S FIRE

Heavenly Father, may we experience that deepest of all joys which is born of holy communion with Thee. Lead us into new fields of our wonderful inheritance in Christ. May we have new surprises of grace. May some fresh revelations of Thy love break upon our astonished vision. Remove the scales from our eyes, so that we may see clearly the things which are waiting to be unveiled. Graciously make known to us what Thou wouldst have us be in order that we may then more clearly apprehend what Thou wouldst have us do. Help us to remember what we ought not to forget, and help us to forget what we ought not to remember. May our minds be the servants of Thy truth. Let the beams of heavenly light chase out the darkness of error and let it be all glorious within. We humbly pray Thee to deliver us from our selfishness, and enlarge and refine our sympathies until they express themselves in willing sacrifice. May we feel the pains of others, and carry their burdens and share their yokes. May the circles of our compassion grow larger every day. Let the ends of the earth be at our own doors, and so may we hear the cry which is very far off. Illumine our lives in this service, and send us forth to enlighten and kindle the lives of others. Make us missionaries of Thy truth and ambassadors of Thy grace and love. May we be quick to discern opportunity, and ready to use it in the service of the King. Amen.

"He shall baptize you with the Holy Ghost and with fire." Matthew 3:11.

Such is the divine promise. Let me read the story of its fulfilment. "And when the day of Pentecost was fully come they were all with one accord in one place. And suddenly there came a sound from heaven as of a rushing mighty wind, and it filled all the house where they were sitting. And there appeared unto them cloven tongues, like as of fire, and it sat upon each of them." Do not let us become victims of the letter and become entangled in the symbolism. It is possible so to regard material signs as to lose their spiritual significance. A musical word may conceal its own thought. Words are purposed to be the vehicles of mind. Symbols are intended to be transparencies, losing themselves in something better. They are ordained to be thoroughfares through which we pass to nobler destinations. The sign is to be the servant of its own significance.

Here then are men and women who are about to receive the promised gift of the Spirit of God. They have been waiting as their Master directed, waiting in prayer, and in prayer incalculably strengthened by community of desire, waiting in trembling watchfulness and expectation. Then the much-hoped-for day arrives and their spirits receive the infinite reinforcement of the gift of the Holy Spirit.

We have a very pale reflection of this experience when two human spirits are given to each other in deep and vital communion. When David received the gift of Jonathan's spirit, and Jonathan received the gift of David's spirit, each of them obtained immeasurable enrichment. When Robert Browning received the gift of Elizabeth Barrett's spirit, and Elizabeth Barrett received the gift of Robert Browning's spirit, who can calculate the wealth which each of them found in the other's possession?

But these examples, and others even more sacred which we could gather from our own experience, are only pale and wan and shadowy, compared with the wonder which breaks upon the soul when the spirit of man receives the gift of the Spirit of God, and the two dwell together in mystic and glorious communion. What happens to the human spirit is suggested to us under the familiar symbols of wind and fire. "Like unto a rushing mighty wind;" "like unto fire." Do not let us be enslaved by any hampering details in the figures. Let us seek their broad significance. And what is the characteristic of a rushing mighty wind? It dispels the fog. It freshens the atmosphere. It gives life and nimbleness to the air. It is the minister of vitality. And the breath of God's Spirit is like that; it clears the human spirit, and freshens it, and vitalizes it; it acts upon the soul like the air of a spiritual spring. And as for the symbol of the fire; fire is the antagonist of all that is frozen; it is the antagonist of the torpid, the tepid; it is the minister of fervour, and buoyancy, and expansion. The wind changes the atmosphere, the fire changes the temperature; and the holy Spirit of God changes the atmosphere and temperature of the soul; and when you have changed the atmosphere and temperature of a soul you have accomplished a mighty transformation. It is about this change in the moral and spiritual temperature that I want to meditate, the gift of fire which we receive in the baptism of the Holy Ghost. If the spirit of man and the spirit of God come into blessed communion, and the fire of God is given, how will it reveal and express itself? For if there be a gift of fire in the soul we shall most surely know it. Fire is one of the things which cannot be hid. You can hide a painted sun in your parlour and no one will know it is there, but you cannot hide a glowing fire. A man can hide a denominational label, he cannot possibly hide the holy fire of God. How, then, shall we know that the fire is there?

First of all I think I should look for the holy fire on the common hearthstone of human love. If the fire of God does not warm up the affections I fail to recognize what its heat can be worth. The first thing to warm up is the heart. The intimate friend of the Holy Spirit is known by the ardour of his affections. He loves with a pure heart fervently. He is baptized with fire. Now I need not seek to prove the existence of cold hearts among us. I am afraid we must accept them without question. Whether there are hearts like fire-grates without a spark of fire I cannot tell. Personally, I have never met with anyone in whose soul the fire of love had gone quite out. I think that if we sought very diligently among the gray dusty ashes of any burnt-out life we should find a little love somewhere. Yes, even in Judas Iscariot, or in the dingy soul-grate of old frozen-out Scrooge. But there are surely souls so cold, and so destitute of love, that the poor fire never leaps up in dancing, cheering, welcome flames. Their temperature is zero.

There are other souls with a little fire of love burning, but it is very sad, very sodden, very sullen, very dull. There is more smoke than fire. There is more surliness than love. Their fire is not inviting and attractive. There is a little spitting, and spluttering, and crackling, but there is no fine, honest, ruddy glow. Their temperature is about ten above freezing. They are not frozen but they are not comforting.

There are other lives where the fire of affection is burning more brightly, and certainly with more attractive glow, but where it seems as if the quality of the fuel must be poor because the fire gives out comparatively little heat. The heart sends out a cheery beam across the family circle, but it does not reach beyond. There is no cordial warmth for the wider circles of fellowship. The fire burns in the home but it does not affect the office. It encompasses the child but it has no cheer for the stranger. What is the temperature of such a life? It is very difficult to appraise it. Perhaps it will be best to say that in one room of the soul the temperature is 60, while in all the other rooms it is down towards freezing.

And, therefore, I need not say how profound is the need in the world for warm, glowing, affectional fires. What awfully cold lives there are in the city, just waiting for the cheer of "the flame of sacred love!" There are souls whose fires have died down at the touch of death. There are others whose glow has been dulled by heavy sorrow. There are others whose love has been slaked by the pitiless rains of pelting defeat. There are others again whose hearts are cold in the midst of material wealth. They have richly furnished dwellings, but their hearts are like ice. They are unloved and unlovely, and they are frostbitten in the realms of luxury. Wealth can buy attention; it can never purchase love. My God! What cold souls there are in this great city!

And, therefore, what a clamant and urgent need there is for love-fires at which to kindle these souls that are heavy, and burdened, and cold. And when the Holy Spirit is given to a man, and he is baptized with fire, it must surely, first of all, be the fire of cordial, human affection. And such is the teaching of experience. When John Wesley came into the fulness of the divine blessing in a little service at Aldersgate Street, London, he said that he "felt his heart strangely warmed." He was receiving the gift of holy fire. And I cannot but think that Charles Wesley was thinking about his brother's experience on that day when he wrote his own immortal hymn which includes the prayerful lines:

"Kindle a flame of sacred love
In these cold hearts of ours."
You find and feel the glow of that love-fire throughout the New Testament Scriptures. They who have the most of God's Spirit have the most of the fire. There was Barnabas, who was declared to be "full of the Holy Spirit," and he is also described as "the son of consolation." What a consummate title! Cannot we feel the love-fire burning and glowing in all his ample ministry? Full of the Spirit, and therefore full of consolation! The truth of the matter is this,—we cannot be much with the Spirit of Christ, and not take fire from His presence. In these high realms, communing is partaking, and we kindle to the same affection as fills the heart of the Lord. "We love because He first loved us." His fire lights our fire, and we burn in kindred passion. So do I proclaim that when the fire of God falls upon our spirits the sacred gift kindles and inflames the soul's affections. When we are baptized with the Holy Ghost and with fire, we receive the glowing power of Christian love.

Where else shall we look for that holy fire in human life? I think I should look for the presence of the fire of the Holy Ghost in fervent enthusiasm for the cause of Christ's Kingdom. And that indeed is what I find. The New Testament instructs me in this, and it teaches me that where man is baptized with the Holy Spirit and with fire his own spirit becomes fervent. He is declared to be "fervent in spirit," and the original word means to bubble up, to boil, as in a boiling kettle; it is the emergence of the mighty power of steam. And so the significance is this: the fire of God generates steam, it creates driving power, it produces forceful and invincible enthusiasm. You will find abundant examples of this spiritual miracle in the Acts of the Apostles; perhaps the Book might be more truly named "The Acts of the Holy Spirit," for all the glorious activity is generated by His holy fire. Let your eyes glance over the apostolic record. Mark how the fire of God endows man with the power of magnificent initiative. Take the apostle Peter;—once his strength was the strength of impulse, a spurt and then a collapse, a spasm and then a retreat, proud beginnings bereft of patience and perseverance. But see him when the Spirit of God has got hold upon him, and what a gift he has received of initial and sustained enthusiasm! "And Peter, filled with the Holy Spirit!" You should see him then, and note the strength of his drive, and the ardour of his enterprise! And the example of Peter would be confirmed by the examples of all the other apostles, if only we knew their personal history and experience. I wish there had been given to us just a glimpse of doubting Thomas, slow, hesitant, reluctant, uncertain, when the Holy Spirit had him in possession. "And Thomas filled with the Holy Spirit,"—I would give something to know the end of that sentence. And I wish we had one glimpse of timid, fearful, night-walking Nicodemus, when the fire of God's Spirit blazed in his soul. "Then Nicodemus, filled with the Holy Spirit,"—I wonder what notable exploits would complete that unfinished sentence. This we know; the holy fire transformed the timid into the courageous, the lukewarm into the fervent, it generated a moral steam which made them invincible.

The first apostles drove through tremendous obstacles. Indeed, they never had the comfort of an open and unimpeded road. Every road was thick with adversaries. What then? Through them or over them! "But, Sire," said a timid and startled officer to Napoleon, on receiving apparently impossible commands, "But, Sire, there are the Alps!" "Then there must be no Alps," replied his audacious chief. "There must be no Alps!" That was the very spirit of the first apostles. Mighty antagonisms reared themselves in their way,—ecclesiastical prejudices, the prejudices of culture, social hostilities, political expediences, and all the subtle and violent contrivances of the world, the flesh and the devil. "But, Sire, there are the Alps!" "There must be no Alps!" Through them! Over them! What that coward Peter got through when the fire of God glowed in his soul! When a man has the holy fire of God within him he has a boiling fervency of spirit, and he can drive through anything.

And that same holy fire gives the same terrific power to-day, the same driving enthusiasm, the same patient, dogged, invincible perseverance. If a man declares that he has received the fire of God's Holy Spirit, I will look eagerly for the impetus of his sacred enthusiasm. If he be a preacher I will look for labour in the passion, and the unsnarable energy and patience which he will assuredly put into his work. If he be a teacher, I will examine the generated steam, and note how much he can do, how far he can travel, and how long he can hold out in the service of his Lord. If he be a man who has set himself to some piece of social reconstruction I will watch with what ardour, and ingenuity, and inevitableness he is moving towards his goal. Is it the smashing of the saloons? "Then Peter, filled with the Holy fire;"—what if that power were harnessed to the enterprise? Or is it the awful plague and blight of impurity; or is it the cleaning up of politics; the establishment of rectitude in civic and national life? Whatever it be, the holy fire of God will reveal its presence in the soul of man in an ardent enthusiasm which cannot be quenched. It is the promise of our God, and shall He not do it? "He maketh His ministers a flaming fire,"—and that fire can never be blown out in the darkest and most tempestuous nights.

And lastly, I shall look for the signs of the presence of the Holy Spirit in the fire of sacred resentment. If a man is baptized with the Holy Ghost, and with fire, I shall expect to see the presence of that fire in the capacity of hot and sensitive indignation. I need not say that there is a mighty difference between hot temper and hot indignation. Hot temper is a firing of loose powder upon a shovel. It is just a flare, and an annoyance, and a danger. But hot indignation is powder concentrated in the muzzle of a gun, and intelligently directed to the overthrow of some stronghold of iniquity. Hot temper is the fire of the devil. Hot indignation is the fire of God; it is the wrath of the Lamb. What is this capacity of indignation? It is the opposite to frozen antipathy, to tepid curiosity, to sinful "don't care," to all immoral coldness and calculated indifference. There are many people who can be irritated, but they are never indignant. They can be offended, but they are never nobly angry. The souls who are possessed with the fire of God are the very opposite to all these. I said at the very beginning of this meditation that the breath of God is like the quickening atmosphere of the Spring; but it is equally true to say that it can be like the destructive blast of the African sirocco—"The grass withereth and the flower fadeth because the Spirit of the Lord bloweth upon it." The hot breath of God is like unto a blast that scorches things in their very roots. And if we share the breath of God's Spirit we too shall be endowed with the ministry of the destructive blast, even the power of a consuming indignation. Any form of public iniquity will make our fire blaze with purifying wrath. Corruption in civic or national government, inhumanity in the treatment of the criminal and the unfortunate, the oppression of the poor, the brutal disregard of the rights of the weak and the defenceless, any one of these will draw out our souls in the hot and aggressive indignation which is the imparted fire of the Holy Ghost. If any one claims to have been baptized with the Holy Ghost and with fire, and he is indifferent in the presence of licensed iniquity, and apathetic and lukewarm when gigantic wrongs glare and stare upon him, that man's spiritual baptism is a pathetic fiction, and his boasted fire is only a painted flame.

But if a man suffer a personal injury, if some wrong is done to him, what kind of fire shall I expect to see in his life if he is filled with the Holy Ghost? Yes, if some one has done an injury to another, and the other has been baptized with the Holy Ghost, what kind of fire will he reveal? Listen to this: "If thine enemy hunger, feed him; if he thirst, give him drink; for in so doing thou shalt heap coals of fire upon his head!" It is the very fire that rains upon us from the Cross of our Lord: "And when they were come to the place which is called Calvary, there they crucified Him, and the malefactors, one on the right hand and the other on the left. Then said Jesus, Father, forgive them, for they know not what they do." What kind of fire is that? It is the same holy fire which flowed from the soul of the martyr Stephen as he was being stoned to death: "Lord, lay not this sin to their charge." It is a marvellous fire, a most arresting fire; and we simply cannot withstand it. It is the very fire of grace; it is live coal from the altar of God.

So this is the sort of fire I look for when a man claims to be filled with the Holy Spirit,—the glowing fire of humble affection, the glowing fire of noble enthusiasm, the glowing fire of indignation, and the marvellous fire of self-forgetting grace. "He shall baptize you with the Holy Ghost and with fire."

"He came in tongues of living flame,
To teach, convince, subdue,
All powerful as the wind He came,
And viewless too.

Spirit of purity and grace,

Our weakness, pitying see,
Oh, make our hearts Thy dwelling-place,
And worthier Thee."

XIII: VICTORY OVER THE BEAST

Heavenly Father, we thank Thee for our knowledge that all our springs are in Thee. Wilt Thou deliver us from any sense of self-dependence, and lead us into an intimate fellowship with the ministers of Thy grace. If any triumph has made us self-confident, if any earthly success has made us proud, may Thy Holy Spirit lead our spirits into the lowliness which is the beginning of true wisdom and strength. We humbly ask that Thou wilt deliver us from the sins which have become our masters, and in which we find unholy delight. Incline our hearts unto Thy law, and help us to find pleasure in obedience to Thy holy will. Graciously redeem us from every care which fetters our souls, and give us such an assurance of Thy providential love that we may exult in the glorious liberty of the children of God. Graciously remember us one by one. Be very near to those who scarcely have the heart to pray. Mercifully meet with those who have been stunned with sorrow, and who have not yet regained the comforts of Thy peace. Remember all who are in grave perplexity, and graciously light Thy lamp on their bewildered way. Receive all our little ones into the circle of Thy blessing, and may they early rejoice in Thy friendship and become devoted to Thy holy will. Amen.

"And I saw as it were a sea of glass mingled with fire: and they that had gotten the victory over the beast." Revelation 15:2.

The symbolism of the city of God as given in the Book of Revelation represents the character of its citizens, and all the glories of the new Jerusalem have correspondences in the souls who live and move in that radiant land. The sea of glass represents a spiritual character of regal serenity, a character transparent in its limpid depths, and reflecting in its stillness the very image of the Lord. And the sea of glass, "mingled with fire," is significant of character made fervent by holy love, purity made genial, righteousness changed into goodness by the permeating heat of affectional enthusiasm and devotion.

And now I wish to examine the next descriptive sentence, which tells us something of the history and experiences of those who have arrived at the sea of glass, and who have attained the serene and genial purity of those who hold immediate communion with God. And this is the sentence which records some of the happenings which have befallen them on the road; "They have gotten the victory over the beast." It is a very striking conjunction, this which tells me that they who dwell by the sea of glass have come by the way of the beast, and that they have conquered the beast by the way. What was the beast which these men and women had faced and conquered as they moved onward to the crystal sea? I do not profess to know the precise historic interpretation. The beast may have been the malignant and vindictive antagonism of the Emperor Nero. He may have been the beast. The beast may have been the hostile and suffocating pressure of the Roman Empire. The beast may have been the stealthy seductions of the imperial city of Rome. The beast may have been the fascinating and paralyzing charm of the world, the flesh, and the devil. Anyone or all of these together may have been the beast which straddled across the road and opposed these Christians on their journey towards home. I do not know, and I frankly confess I am not deeply concerned to know. The general boldness of the figure is quite enough for me. Whatever else the beast may mean it must essentially mean anti-God, anti-Christ, the antagonist of the divine. It must mean the animal side of our nature seeking to invade the realm of the spirit, to force its way among the executive powers of the soul, and to usurp the throne of God. The beast is triumphant when the flesh and all the works of the flesh have ousted the forces of the spirit. The beast is conquered when the powers of the spirit never surrender their holy sovereignty, when the forces of the flesh have been ordered to their place among the rank and file, and when they are never allowed to wear the honours and prerogatives of the commander-in-chief. "They that have gotten the victory over the beast." The beast is just anti-Christ, in whatever form he may appear.

Let us spend a little while in first of all examining this beast who claims the control and mastery of our souls. Everybody has a vivid experience of his power, but it may help to clarify our minds if we consider what has been said about him by the recognized masters and counsellors of the soul. Let us turn, then, to the pages of literature, and first of all let us turn to the inspired literature itself. You have scarcely opened the Word of God before the beast makes his appearance in the form of a serpent. "Now the serpent was more subtle than any beast of the field." And who has not experienced the wiles of the serpent when he approaches the soul in some charming seduction, in some fascinating crookedness, in some wriggling sophistry, in some twisted excuse, in some winding compromise? Who has not seen the beast when he has sought to persuade the soul that the wriggle is the most graceful form of motion, and that the curve is more acceptable than the straight line? Who has not heard him when he has argued that the detour is the shortest way home, and that a slight deviation from rectitude will lead to the noblest ends? Yes, this beast is the apostle of the serpentine, and this is his creed,—the wriggle is the best way to your goal. "The serpent was more subtle than any beast of the field."

I turn over the pages of the old book, and I am confronted with an extraordinary change in the form of the beast. He is no longer a wriggling serpent but a prowling lion. "The devil goeth abroad like a roaring lion." He no longer makes a seductive approach to the intellect with his advocacy of the crooked way; he makes a passionate assault upon the spirit with all the fiery forces of the flesh. It is no longer the wriggle but a terrific leap. And who has not known him in this wild approach? It is just the tremendous weight and pounce of anti-spiritual impulse, the mighty onrush of carnal longing and desire. The lion is sheer mass and weight of hungry craving. Who has not known the lion in the way?... And yet beside the crystal sea are those "who have gotten the victory over the beast."

Again I turn over the pages of the old book, and once again the form of the beast has changed and he appears before me in the guise of a fox. It is our Master's name for the foe. And who has not known the beast when he has assailed the soul in the manner of a fox? It is the assault of cunning, when things are made to appear in semblance what they are not in spirit and in truth. Nay, it is the very art of foxiness that the fox itself is made to look like a goose, and the wolf is given the appearance of a lamb. Vice is dressed up like virtue. Falsehood moves about in white robes and innocently accosts us in the dress of a white lie. License tricks itself out as gaiety. Sin clothes itself in the fashions of the hour and hides its talons in silks. I say this is the very genius of the fox,—he makes you think you are having converse with a harmless old goose! Who has not known the fox when he cunningly tried to persuade us that the devil was God, and that hell was heaven, and that death was.... But, O no, he never mentions death! In his scheme it is part of the trick that death shall never be known. The old fox! And yet, in spite of fox and lion and serpent, there were those beside the sea of glass "who had gotten the victory over the beast."

Let me lead you further, for a moment or two, into the pages of a wider literature, and let it be into the pages of Dante and John Bunyan. In his immortal book Dante tells us that when he turned his feet to the pilgrim road he was successively confronted by three beasts which sought to stop his journey. And first he met a leopard:

"And lo! just as the sloping side I gained,
A leopard, subtle, lithe, exceeding fleet,
Whose skin full many a dusky spot did stain;
Nor did she from before my face retreat;
Nay, hindered so my journey on the way,
That many a time I backward turned my feet."

The leopard which confronted Dante was the symbol of sensuous beauty which sought to block his road and ensnare his feet. Next he was confronted by a lion:

"Yet o'er me, spite of this, did terror creep—
From aspect of a lion drawing near.
He seemed as if upon me he would leap,
With head upraised and hunger fierce and wild,
So that a shudder through the air did sweep."

The lion was to Dante the symbol of worldly pride. And next he met a wolf:

"A she-wolf, with all ill-greed defiled,
Laden with hungry leanness terrible."

And the wolf was to Dante the lean symbol of a hungry greed; it was the beastly type of avarice. And who has not shared the experience of Dante on his own road and encountered the leopard, the lion and the wolf?... And yet there were those before the sea of glass who had got the victory over the beast.

Turn to John Bunyan. There is a wonderful passage in the early part of John Bunyan's "Holy War," in which he describes the preparations which the beast has made for his attack upon the soul. He tells how beast held counsel with beast, and how it was agreed that they should assume forms with which the soul was quite familiar; such as were accounted harmless, lest the soul should be alarmed when they made their deadly approach. "Therefore let us assault the soul in all pretended fairness, covering our intentions with all manner of lies, flatteries, and illusive words; feigning things that will never be, and promising that to them which they shall never find." And so they marched toward the soul, "all in a manner invisible," save only one, and he took on a shape as harmless and familiar as a bird, and when he spoke he spake with such gentleness "as if he had been a lamb." And I for one put myself side by side with John Bunyan, for I too have known the beast when he has come disguised, and has addressed me with all the harmlessness and innocence of a lamb.

I will add one further word in our consideration of the beast. When I look around on the world to-day, upon the appalling scenes of passion and hatred and slaughter,—it is to me very significant that so many of the national emblems, which represent the corporate life of peoples, are different types of beasts. It is the beast which still provides the symbols of our national life. There is the lion; there is the bear; there is the wolf, and I know not what besides! We talk of rousing the bear and of twisting the lion's tail! Our national emblems are beasts. The American nation has happily discarded the beast, but it has chosen one of the fiercest among the birds—the bird whose talons are more obtrusive than its song. I am suggesting the significance of the fact that we have found nothing above the beast to symbolize the individuality of national life. Perhaps some day we may "move upward," and we may erase the beasts from our emblems, but it will only be when we have driven the beasts from our souls!

Well, then, after this swift glimpse into inspired and general literature, and this glance upon the typical symbols of the national life, we are more disposed than ever to say that the beast is just anti-Christ, the presumptuous claim of the animal to take the place of the spiritual, the defiant claim of the devil to usurp the throne of God. But here are men and women whose triumph is recorded in my text, who have conquered the beast, and who have attained a strong and fervent purity in which the spirit is all in all. What was the secret of their triumph? By what means and ministries did they conquer the beast? Happily we are left in no manner of doubt, and the means by which they conquered are offered to you and me. What says the Old Book?—"They overcame by the blood of the Lamb." Let us tell their secret very quietly and very simply, without any waste of words,—they shared the blood of Jesus Christ and it changed them into giants. In some way or other a communion was formed between their life and His life, and His mighty life flowed into their life as vine-blood flows into the branch of the vine. They shared the strength of Him who fought the beast in the wilderness of Judea, and who fought him again in still more alluring forms in the courts of Jerusalem and by the shores of the Lake of Galilee. Yes, if you had asked these radiant victors by the sea of glass to tell you how they triumphed, they would have reverently turned their faces towards the Lord and eagerly answered, "By the blood of the Lamb!"

"I asked them whence their victory came,
They with united breath
Ascribed their conquest to the Lamb,
Their triumph to His death."

And the second secret of their triumph is to be found in their continual warfare. They drank his blood to fight his fights. It is a fight that knows no armistice. It acknowledges no flag of truce. Eternal vigilance and eternal struggle is the price of spiritual freedom. Life is warfare; it is never parade-drill; it is never holiday review; we are never off duty; the contest is constant, and the close of every day records a victory or a defeat. Our Master never promised his soldiers a life of ease. The beast promises roads which are pleasant as field paths that lead through grassy meadows. There shall be no flints, no thorns, no briars; and if we choose, we can lie down in the meadows morning, noon and night! That is the promise that the beast makes,—a promise which is always broken. Our Lord always calls us to battles, to noble crusades and prolonged campaigns. "His blood-red banner streams afar!" He calls us to share the travail that makes His Kingdom come. Yes, He calls us to glorious, endless battles, but He promises sure and certain victory if we drink His blood along the way.

And so they conquered the beast by the blood of the Lamb. They conquered by the continual battles of their faith. And lastly they conquered by their songs of victory. They sang their way to the sea of glass, and their songs were songs of victory all along the road. They did not moan in misereres; they did not wail in lamentations as if the beast were mightier than their Lord. They knew their Lord was mightier than all; and their songs of victory were the beginning of their triumph. O, the singing that abounds in the Word of God! O, the singing you may hear in the Acts of the Apostles! And, O, the singing that sounds through the Book of Revelation; the song of victory, the song of Moses and the Lamb! At the battle of Dunbar, in the great critical days of English freedom, Cromwell's troops sang their way to victory. They could hear the roaring of the sea. The land was swept with deluges of rain. But above the roar of the sea, and the sound of the pelting rain, they lifted their voices in praise to God, and as they swept into battle their song rang out; "God is our refuge and strength, a very present help in time of trouble; therefore will we not fear if the earth be removed and the mountains be shaken in the heart of the seas! The Lord of Hosts is with us; the God of Jacob is our refuge!" Their song was part of their armour; it was indeed like that word of the Christian, Appollinaris, in Ibsen's play,—"The Emperor Julian," which he spake when the forces of the beast were massed against the soldiers of the cross;—"Verily I say unto you, so long as song rings out above our sorrows, Satan shall never conquer!" Verily, I too will say that our praise is an invincible armour,—we sing our way to the triumph we seek!

Men and women, the beast can be conquered, for the mouth of the Lord hath spoken it! You and I may stand at the sea of glass, pure, transparent, fervent with divine love, victors over the beast, through the blood of the Lamb, through constancy in battle, and in songs which ring out above our sorrows, as we push along life's way.

"Soldiers of Christ, arise!
And put your armour on;
Strong in the strength which God supplies
Through His eternal Son.

From strength to strength go on,
Wrestle, and fight and pray;
Tread all the powers of darkness down
And win the well-fought day."

XIV: THE COMING GOLDEN AGE

Holy Father, we thank Thee for the privilege of fellowship, and for the help which we can give to one another. May the faith of everyone be strengthened by the faith of all. May our penitence be deepened because we are all engaged in common confession. May our joys be enriched because we are all contemplating the unsearchable riches of Christ. May our obedience become more devoted because we all drink of the waters of inspiration. Impart unto us the grace of sacred sympathy. May we reverently bear one another's burdens and carry them in the arms of intercession. We beseech Thee to grant unto us visions of Thy glory in so far as our eyes are able to bear them. May we make new discoveries among the mysteries of Thy truth. May the whole worship prepare us for a larger ministry in the service of Thy kingdom. Wilt Thou give us the armor we need for the great campaign. Especially may we receive the endowment of the love that never grows faint. Reveal to us our work, and then lead us into a devotion which will never be satisfied until the work is finished. Look upon the whole world in this hour of desolation and woe. Enlarge our hearts to comprehend the sorrow, and may we share the sufferings of our Lord in sacrificial labors. Let Thy kingdom come, O Lord, and let Thy will be done on earth as it is in heaven. Amen.

"And many people shall go up and say, Come ye and let us go up to the mountain of the Lord, to the house of the God of Jacob; and he will teach us of his ways, and we will walk in his paths: for out of Zion shall go forth the law, and the word of the Lord from Jerusalem. And he shall judge among the nations, and shall rebuke many people: and they shall beat their swords into ploughshares, and their spears into pruning-hooks: nation shall not lift up sword against nation, neither shall they learn war any more." Isaiah 2: 3, 4.

There is something almost unreal in these words when they are read aloud in the times through which we are passing. They sound like the voice of a mocking-bird calling from the midst of the dust and the débris of a ruined world. It is like hearing the gentle peal of church bells on the bloody field of battle. It is like anything you choose which has become unreal, and which has been transferred from the healthy book of noble prophecy to the bitter pages of satire and the sour lips of the cynic. Yes, I grant that the great passage unfolds ideals which have become mere scraps of paper, torn and retorn into a thousand pieces, and blown about like withered leaves in an autumn gale. What, then, are we to do? I am reminded of what Lord Morley said in Manchester a few weeks ago. "When the war is ended,—this mournful chapter of sore bereavement and wasted treasure, when all that is gone, I ask is there not a moral loss which ought to be counted, a moral loss in the wreck of ideals in which the men of my generation were deeply concerned? That loss has got to be counted and retrieved. The fabric of those ideals has to be built up again in the hearts and minds of men and women." Surely that is an opportune word, and it offers both counsel and warning to the Christian Church. We must not just sit down in the bloody dust, and wail our misereres in deadly impotence. We have got to reconstruct the ruined pile, and we must begin the reconstruction by rebuilding the golden palace of our dreams.

And if we are going to rear again that stately temple of vision and dream, who can give us nobler help than the Hebrew prophets, and who among the prophets can help us more than Isaiah? Isaiah was a prophet interpreting the mind of God. He was a statesman with a keen and comprehensive outlook on human affairs. He was also a poet bringing to human problems the illuminating imagination of the seer. He lived in a time of grave national disloyalties, a time when peoples were abandoning their most sacred trust. His were days of international strife and convulsion, days witnessing vast world movements in which empires were seen at their birth, and empires were seen in withering decline and death. Isaiah was a man whose thought was distinguished by breadth and depth and length. He saw things broadly, he saw things deeply, and he also saw the things which gleamed afar. And as he looked out upon the world to his vision the troubled and chaotic day merged into a reconstituted order of active concord and peace. Isaiah was a confirmed optimist. He had a keen sense of the future. He felt the days before him. He could scent the waving harvest while yet the snow was on the ground. He could catch the sound of harvest-home while the wintry wind was whistling across the ice-bound field. And looking out over the dark scene of convulsion and disaster, and amid the rude and brutal clamour of international strife, he sang this song of the morning,—"They shall beat their swords into ploughshares, and their spears into pruning-hooks; nation shall not lift up sword against nation, neither shall they learn war any more." If we are purposing to rebuild the fallen ideals of our own day, and so reconstruct our common life, can we do better than stand near this man for guidance and inspiration?

How, then, does this man say that the golden dream is to be realized? Through what preparatory stages are we to pass before we reach the shining consummation? Isaiah declares that the fulfilment of the dream is to begin in the profound revival of spiritual religion. "It shall come to pass in the latter days that the mountain of the Lord's house shall be established at the head of the mountains, and shall be exalted above the hills." That is to say, the dominant peak in the reconstructed landscape is to be a shining spirituality of pure and undefiled religion. Man's relationship to God is to be the supreme relation overtopping and overseeing everything else. "And many peoples shall say, Come ye, and let us go up to the mountain of the Lord, to the house of the God of Jacob, and He will teach us of His ways, and we will walk in His paths." That is to say, in the golden age this is to be the common aspiration; spiritual desire and spiritual ambition are to be dominant; the biggest thing in life is to be the yearning for the divine communion, the gladsome craving for fellowship in the heavenly quest. That is how the golden dream is to begin to be fulfilled; it is to begin in the recovery of vital worship, in the profound revival of spiritual religion.

Now, all the best things can be mimicked in the cheapest counterfeits! Pearls can be so skilfully manufactured that even the expert eye can be deceived. There are diamonds about, common as window glass, and their dancing gleams can delude the very elect. Yes, the best things can be cleverly imitated, and their counterfeits can move unsuspected in the most exalted places. It would be an amusing trait, if it were not a tragic characteristic of human nature, how willing we are to borrow the clothes of realities, and just strut about in our cheap and glittering attire. And it is so easily done! Anybody can borrow the jolly meters of Rudyard Kipling and put their own tawdry stuff into his caskets; and a thousand people have done it! Anybody can borrow the disorderly irregularities of Walt Whitman, and into his eccentric bottles they can pour their own cheap wine; and crowds of people have done it! It is so easy to borrow clothes, and bottles, and outer forms. Yes, and it is so easy to borrow the outer garments of religion and to move about in the mere trappings of devotion. We can borrow the sacramental cup and put into it the thinnest and the most diluted wine of life. Our apparent religion can be just an affair of clothes, a borrowed skin, an acted thing, a play, a theatricality with feigned postures and emotions, altogether devoid of blood-red life, and having no deep and vital commerce with the Infinite. Religion can be conventional, having no inner sanction of fine awe and godly fear. We can get religion while all the time religion has not got us. It can be just a light performance, a social convention and not a solemn travail in which the soul is doing great business in deep waters in communion with the eternal God.

Now, is not this the religious condition into which the world has drifted in these latter days? I do not make exception of any country, not even of America. This country is delivered from the horrors of the European convulsion, not by a separating gulf of moral and spiritual condition, but by 3,000 miles of sea. If the coast line of America had been twenty-five miles from the coast of Europe she would have been involved in the woes of the boiling cauldron. And therefore do I put the inclusive question,—and I venture to challenge your judgments,—is not the religious condition which I have suggested one into which the entire Christian world appears to have fallen? Multitudes of Christian people are just wearing the clothes of religion. We have religious professions without spiritual possessions. We have religious conventionality without devotional vitality. We have the show without the life. We have the skin of religion without its sacrificial heart. We have the crucifix without the Saviour. We have the altar but not the open heaven.

You may make the test in any way you please. Let us test our condition by any one of the primary characteristics of true and vital religion. Let us apply one test. Let us test our condition by our own secret and personal communion with the Lord. I am speaking in a Christian church, and I am addressing professedly Christian people; well, how do we stand the test? What proportion of the members of the Church of Christ in this country have a really living and fruitful fellowship with God? How many have walked the way of communion so frequently that it is now a much-beloved and well-trodden road, along which they can easily and naturally make their way in the dark, yea, even in the stormy midnight when the floods are out, and the tempest howls about their ways?

For we cannot have religion with God wiped out! If religion is only beneficence, if it is only decent, respectable living, if it is only a comfortable conformity with accepted social standards,—if that is all it is, then let us say so and have done with it. Let us pull down our altars and fling their useless stones to the winds. But this is not religion. True religion is more than this. True religion is the reverent and most solemn recognition of the eternal God. It is the conscious prostration of the soul in His most holy Presence. It is the free because reverent fellowship of a child with the Father. It is the loyal acceptance of the Father's will. It is the humble reception of His grace as offered to us in Jesus Christ our Lord. It is the assumption of our life as a sacred trust accepted from the hands of God. It is the anticipation of His glory in our eternal home. Religion has great human relationships with our fellowman, and these shall not be overlooked. But for the moment, I am speaking of the fontal relationship of the soul with God, that fundamental fellowship in which all other worthy fellowships are born, and I ask you whether all the peoples of all professing Christian nations have not wandered far from the vitalizing bond of this primary communion? Let your eyes roam over the darkened world; dense clouds are still rising everywhere on the ominous horizon. How is that night-time to be turned into day, yea, into a day like unto a lovely summer's morning? Here is the answer of the greatest of the prophets when he, too, was confronted with tempest and night;—the first thing we have to pray for, and work for, and seek for, in every Christian country, is a profound revival of spiritual religion, when "the mountain of the Lord's house shall be established at the head of the mountains, and when many peoples shall say, Let us go up to the mountain of the Lord, and He will teach us of His ways, and we will walk in His paths." This, I say, is needed in every country, until in every country all who profess the Saviour's name shall cry out in the fervour of a great and quenchless desire,—"As the hart panteth after the water brook, so panteth my soul after Thee, O God!"

Now look at the second stage in the realization of the golden dream. "He will teach us of His ways, and we will walk in His paths.... And He shall judge between the nations." That is to say, a profound revival of spiritual religion will be accompanied by loftier and more exacting moral standards. He will teach and we will walk. Morals always grow lax when piety gets cool. When religion becomes a mere conventionality, morality always loses its awful sanctions. Wipe out God and your moral standards will surely fall. If I neglect the temperature of my greenhouse, or if I play fast and loose with it, my tender plants will assuredly droop. And if I neglect my spiritual temperature, which is the climate of my soul, my moral and spiritual flowers will be smitten and pinched. We cannot lower our spirituality and yet have our morality keep its winsome bloom. Let me ask you,—have you ever known anyone grow loose and careless in their religion, and at the same time become correspondingly nobler and purer, and more scrupulously faithful in their daily life? Have you ever known anyone drop Christ and then become more like Him? Have you ever had occasion to whisper this secret concerning any living woman,—"O, yes, she broke off communion with Christ, and then she put on moral grace and beauty like a robe?" The very question is an insult to our intelligence, as it is an affront to our experience; for this is the eternal law, whose workings can be witnessed every day,—when the spirit deteriorates the moral life becomes diseased.

On the other hand, let there be an enrichment in vital godliness and our conduct will begin to shine like burnished gold. "He will teach," says the prophet, "and we will walk." He, with Whom we hold vital communion, He will be the teacher of the spirit, and the illuminant of the conscience and the inspiration of the will; a nobler conduct will be born of that fellowship as surely as the choicest grapes are the children of the healthiest vines. When we are all in living and deep communion with Christ, truly worshipping in the innermost secret place,—English, and German, and American, and Japanese,—a finer spirit of judgment will be abroad in the earth, a healthier moral climate, and we shall naturally and instinctively seek to do what Jesus did, and in the way that Jesus did it, when He came and dwelt among us as a carpenter's Son, Son of Mary, Son of Man, Son of God!

Only one thing remains to be said as to the process by which the radiant dream of the prophet is to be fulfilled. When there has come a profound revival of spiritual religion, and, consequently, a loftier and more exacting moral standard, there will be a wonderful conversion of destructive forces in the personal and national life. "They shall beat their swords into ploughshares and their spears into pruning-hooks." I want you carefully to notice that the sword is not to be destroyed; it is to be transformed; it is to become a ploughshare. The spear is not to be broken and thrown away; it is to be converted into a pruning-hook. That is to say, the rudely destructive energies in human life are to be changed into constructive energies. What was darkly negative is to become brightly positive. The martial is to be transformed into the pastoral. The rude implement of slaughter is to become the breaker of the earth-clod or the helpful friend of the vine. "They shall beat their swords into ploughshares and their spears into pruning-hooks." After the first historic siege of Antwerp, the cannon balls were taken and converted into church bells; and may the gracious and holy Lord grant that there may speedily come such a transformation in modern Antwerp, when all the ministers of carnage shall be changed into sweet and sacred ministers of worship and devotion!

But now, if swords are to be beaten into ploughshares and spears into pruning-hooks, where must that work begin? It must begin in the individual heart. We are never going to get the swords out of the nations until we have got them out of the hearts. There is a sword in the heart, a cruel sword, a minister of destruction. There is a sword in the German heart, and a sword in the English heart, and a sword in the American heart, and that sword has got to be transformed before the material sword can become a ploughshare of the field! We are all familiar with our own swords; perhaps I had better say, we are all acquainted with one another's swords. There is the sword of ill-will. There is the spear of deadly gossip. There is the sword of evil prejudice. There is the spear of petty spite and contempt. Yea, surely there is a sordid armoury in the soul. And this has to be converted into a tool-house of a noble Christian culture before the material armouries can be emptied and the sound of war is heard no more.

And therefore, the great national revolution is to begin in individual conversions, and these are to be the children of a vital and saving religion. The transformation of the world is to begin in the conversion of people like you and me. There is no other way. When our own militaristic armour, the one stored in our own soul, is changed into a garden tool-house,—malice changed into good-will, suspicion into enlightened understanding, cynicism into genial and gracious esteem, and foul hatred into Christ's own strong and fruitful love, then we are bringing the day nearer of which the herald angels sang, when there shall be "peace on earth and good will among men."

All this cannot be done by scholarship. We cannot do it by legislation. We cannot do it by commerce. It is the vital work of salvation, and it only can be done by the Saviour of the world. And He must do it in His own way, and His work must be thorough, profound, fundamental. He must search the very cellarings of our being, seeking out our wickednesses as with a candle, and cleansing and purifying us in the deepest and most secret rooms of the soul. And when we thus come to know our Saviour, we shall most surely come to know our brother, for we shall see him with ourselves in the radiant light of the same eternal grace and love. Then will our swords be beaten into ploughshares and our spears into pruning-hooks and we shall learn war no more!

XV: MORE THAN CONQUERORS

Heavenly Father, wilt Thou graciously redeem us from any perilous mood of independence which sets our wills against Thine. Help us to find ourselves in Thee, and to come to our inheritance in the riches of Thy grace. Give us that lowliness of spirit which will enable us to find the gate of higher life and to enter in. Forgive the sin that binds our judgment and enable us through a pure heart to see ourselves in Christ, and to behold ourselves perfected in the power of His love. Save us from low ideals. Lift us out of the thoughts that belittle us and which check and destroy our powers of growth. Give us wider and deeper conceptions of all things. May the experiences of our life come to us as helpful disciplines, through which we may apprehend more of Thy purpose, and more swiftly put on the likeness of our Lord. May we not be mastered by our circumstances, but may we be so strong in Thy strength, that every circumstance may be our servant, adding some fresh grace to our spirits, and some new influence to our lives. May we lose the things we ought not to keep, and may we desire the things we ought to find. Control us, O Lord, by Thy spirit, taking us away from the shallows of common life into the great deep privileges of communion with Thee. Amen.

"In all these things, we are more than conquerors." Rom. 8:37.

Was the writer of these words himself a conqueror? To whom is he making the proud boast? He is writing his letter to the people of Rome. And it is in this letter to Rome that the apostle claims to be a conqueror. If he had been writing to a little company of people living in some quiet and remote district in Asia Minor, far away from the movement and pageantry of imperial life, his boast of being a conqueror might have been received without surprise. But think of the daring of making his claim in a letter to the Romans, who were accustomed to gaze upon their conquerors as they returned in glory from triumphant wars of conquest, dragging their distinguished captives at their chariot wheels! When the apostle claims to be a conqueror he is using a word which to the Romans is weighted with pomp and glory, suggesting cities ablaze with emblems of festivity, and streets thronged with cheering multitudes, and a hero upon whom favours are being showered thick as the flowers which are flung upon his triumphal car. When Paul dares to call himself a conqueror in a letter to the Romans he is using a word significant of all this wealth and effulgence, and he is using it to describe the passage of his own life down the ways of time. "We are more than conquerors." Such a claim would surely strike the Roman reader with amazement.

What was there in the apostle's life to correspond to the claim? What was there about it which in any way recalled the radiant entry of an acclaimed warrior into the festive city of Rome? Let us glance at the external circumstances of his Christian life. Is there anything in these circumstances of pomp, and flowers, and favour, and acclamation? Run your eye over the apostle's road. What are its features? What is it like as it stretches from Damascus to Rome? In peril of his life in Damascus, his enemies watching the gates day and night to kill him; coldly suspected by his fellow-believers in Jerusalem; persecuted at Antioch; assaulted in Iconium; stoned in Lystra; beaten with many stripes in Philippi; attacked by a lewd and envious crowd in Thessalonica; pursued by callous enmity in Berea; despised in Athens; blasphemed in Corinth and dragged before the judgment-seat; exposed to the fierce wrath of the Ephesians; bound with chains in Jerusalem, and finally imprisoned at Rome! Such is the character of his cold, storm-swept, painful road. And yet he dares to call himself a conqueror, and to so style himself to the men of imperial Rome! When I turn away from the gay and rapturous streets, through which the Roman conqueror made his tumultuous entry, and then gaze on the long, dark, cruel road on which this man trudged throughout all his public days, his life seems to be broken up in successive tragedies, and to sink at last in the black defeat of utter and complete eclipse. And yet he sings aloud in joyful pride: "We are more than conquerors"! Where, then, shall we look for the signs of conquest, and for the waving banners, and the rapturous shouts?

There are two ways of estimating a triumphant life. We may trace the line of external circumstances, and we make an inventory of the material treasures, and the flattering diplomas, and the public honours that have been gained along the way. That road winds by the bank, and the Stock Exchange, through Wall Street, or Threadneedle Street, and thence it stretches away through fair suburbs of material comforts, and through gardens of enticing ease, ascending even to lofty eminences of public favour and regard. We may walk along this road in our desire to estimate a man's standing, and to reckon the degree and quality of his conquests. And judged by that standard Paul's circumstances were disastrous, and his life was just a dismal succession of appalling defeats. Indeed the apostle himself has given his own verdict upon his life when it is judged by the standard of Wall Street, and he has done it in two words of pregnant and sweeping brevity—"having nothing"! And yet he claimed to be "more than conqueror"!

But there is another way of judging the failure or triumph of a life. We may follow the line of character. We may register the success of the soul in its mastery of circumstances, in its refusal to be submerged by evil antagonisms, in its preservation of a diamond-like translucency amid engulfing floods of defilement, in its buoyancy in the days of prolonged disappointment, in its quiet and firm ascendency over the beast, in its inevitable emergence from every kind of hostility in increasing majesty and strength. These are the two lines of investigation. These are the possible criteria of judgment. On the one hand we may measure the success of a life by the progressive enrichment of circumstances; on the other hand we may estimate its conquests by the progressive growth of the soul. We may make our valuation in the material world or in the spiritual world; that is to say, we may value the man or we may value his possessions.

Now the circumstantial happenings in a life had little or no interest for the apostle Paul. All his concern followed the inward line of the spirit. He kept his eyes on spiritual processes and never on material results. He did not busy himself with a man's happenings; he busied himself with the effect of the happenings on the man. Always and everywhere he pressed through condition to character; his thought always took the short cut to the soul. If in the streets of Rome or of Ephesus you had pointed out to him some rich man, Paul would have immediately leaped the adjective and inquired about the noun. He would have had no interest whatever in the man's riches; riches are no criterion of triumph; but he would have been devouringly interested in what the riches had done with the man. While the man has been making riches, what have riches made of the man? Measure the man! Is the man who is within the riches a victor or a victim, a noble master or a poor ignoble slave.

And so also do I believe that if you had pointed out to the apostle some poor man, he would have left the adjective and fixed upon the noun. What about the man inside the poverty? What about the soul so ill-housed in indigence? Is the soul royal or servile? Is it crouching or has it a noble and stately rectitude? That would be the concern of the apostle Paul. He would get behind the riches to the man. He would get behind the poverty to the man. For every external happening or every material possession is only a house, and within the happening there is the man or the woman, the tenant of the house. What about them? What about the quality of their manliness or womanliness? That was the apostle's line of investigation. The apostle Paul was not much concerned about the character of the road, whether it was bare or flowery, but he was vitally concerned with the spiritual condition of the traveller. How is it with the pilgrim soul? What spiritual conquests has the soul made along the road? That is the apostle's standard of measurement, and by its records he registers life's conquests or defeats.

Well, then, what was the quality of his own life when it is measured by these interior standards? For, after all, these are the only standards worth naming, as in our sober and thoughtful moments we all very well know. We are not here to make fortunes, we are here to grow souls. How then does the apostle bear the supreme test of his own spiritual standards? Is he master or slave? Are the streets of his soul festive with triumph, or are they dull and cheerless in defeat? Is he more than conqueror?

Let us begin the test with a day when his external circumstances were brilliant. Brilliant days came but rarely to the apostle Paul; they were as infrequent as oases in Sahara's thirsty waste. Test him then on one of his rare, brilliant days, for the dazzling circumstance is often our severest test. Some souls shrivel in the bright sunshine. They grow less in their enlarging circumstances as some nut-kernels contract in the expanding shell. Here is Paul on a great day, when by the mighty grace of God he has made an impotent man to walk. How is the deed regarded? What does the crowd think about him? Listen to the records: "And when the people saw what Paul had done, they lifted up their voices, saying in the speech of Lycaonia, The gods are come down to us in the likeness of men. And they called Barnabas, Jupiter; and Paul, Mercurius, because he was the chief speaker. Then the priest of Jupiter, which was before their city, brought oxen and garlands unto the gates, and would have done sacrifice with the people." How now? The public favour is dazzling! What about the man inside the dazzling happenings? Is the man contracting in pride or is his soul expanding in humility? "Which, when the apostles, Barnabas and Paul, heard of, they rent their clothes, and ran in among the people, crying out, and saying, Sirs, why do ye these things? We also are men of like passions with you, and preach unto you that ye should turn from these vanities unto the living God, which made heaven, and earth, and the sea, and all things that are therein." Do you mark that? This man shines in the sunshine. Popular favour made him kneel before his God, and God's gentleness made him great. The circumstances did not lessen him. His soul did not shrivel and wither in the popular blaze. His soul grew larger, and the man mastered his circumstances; he was bigger than his blazing fate, he was "more than conqueror."

But I have said that brilliant days were rare with the apostle Paul: Let us test him, then, when his days were frowning, when the clouds were lowering, and when his circumstances nipped him like the winter frosts. Does his soul expand in the winter, or does it shrink like frostbitten fruit? Take this little glimpse of one of his days: "And there came to Lystra certain Jews from Antioch and Iconium, who persuaded the people, and, having stoned Paul, drew him out of the city, supposing he had been dead." Having stoned Paul, they dragged him out of the city. How swift and red is the record! Did he grow hard in the stoning? Did he become small and petty and peevish and revengeful? Let me read to you: "And when they had preached the gospel to that city, and had taught many, they returned again to Lystra, and to Iconium, and Antioch, confirming the souls of the disciples, and exhorting them to continue in the faith, and that we must through much tribulation enter into the Kingdom of God." This man's fruit grew sweeter at the touch of the frost. This soul grew larger in the season of apparent defeat. He was "more than conqueror."

Look again through this window. Here is a very dark and bitter happening: "And when they had laid many stripes upon them, they cast them into prison, charging the jailer to keep them safely: who, having received such a charge, thrust them into the inner prison, and made their feet fast in the stocks." How now? Will this man Paul scowl in the darkness? Will his magnanimity sour into the bitter mood of revenge? Listen to the record: "And at midnight Paul and Silas prayed, and sang praises unto God: and the prisoners heard them." Do you mark that? This man was a victim but he was also a victor. We almost forget his sufferings in the sound of his praise. Adversity did not rob him of his crown. He was "more than conqueror."

And so I might go on introducing instance after instance, in every record of his turbulent life, showing how he attained to magnificent mastery in the spirit. When Paul speaks of being a "conqueror" he means that he is on the top of his circumstances and not beneath them. To be more than conqueror is to be on the top of your wealth and not beneath it; to be on the top of your poverty and not beneath it; to be on the top of your joy and not beneath it; to be on the top of your sorrow and not beneath it; to be on the top of your disappointment and not beneath it. To be more than conqueror is to be on the top of the old serpent, and, as Browning says, to stand upon him and to feel him wriggle beneath your feet! The real conqueror, the only one worthy of that royal name, is he who makes every circumstance his subject, permitting no circumstance to be the lord and master of his soul. He is "more than conqueror."

And what is the secret of such conquest? Here is the secret: "We are more than conquerors through Christ that loved us." It is conquest through the energy of an imparted love. Nay, it is much more than that. It is conquest through humble yet intimate communion with the eternal Lover. You remember what conquests the knights of the olden time could achieve when they were conscious that love-eyes were fixed upon them in the jousts. And if this were so with knights of ancient chivalry, when love inspired them in the fray, how infinitely more must it be so with the knights of King Jesus' Order when they know that the love-eyes of the Lord are always fixed upon them in the field! "He loved me" sings the greatest of the apostolic knights. "He loved me and gave Himself for me." What tremendous exploits of patience and of service lie latent in that supreme assurance!

For, mark you, all love conveys the lover to the beloved. The very secret of love is self-impartation to the beloved. Love can never content herself with the gifts of things. Charity gives things. Love always gives herself. Yes, the lover gives herself! And if love is thus self-giving tell me, then, what inconceivable giving is wrapped up in the love of Christ for Paul, and in the love of Christ for thee and me? In an infinitely deeper and richer sense than ever a loving bridegroom gives himself to his loving bride, our great and gracious Lover, the Christ, gives Himself to all who will receive Him. The Saviour's love is the giving of Himself.

Shall I now dare to put that vast and awe-inspiring content into my text? Listen again to the text: "We are more than conquerors through Christ who loved us." Now hear it: "We are more than conquerors through Him who has given himself to us." That word expresses the very gospel of His grace. The Christian believer faces all his circumstances, not merely with a love but with a Lover, and with a Lover who Himself mastered every circumstance, and was the conqueror of sin and death. So this is how the Gospel music rings: "We are more than conquerors through Him the Conqueror"! By reverent faith we share His very love, we drink His very blood, and all our circumstances are made to pay tribute to the health and welfare of our souls. We are more than conquerors through Him Who is ever riding forth, conquering, and to conquer.

Now I think I can go back to those streets of Rome where we began, and where we watched the triumphant conqueror returning home with his spoils. And now I am not surprised at Paul's daring to use the glowing word "Conqueror" to portray the glorious victories of the soul. When I go into the realm of his soul the roadway is lined with a cheering multitude; he is "compassed about with a great cloud of witnesses." A blood-red banner is waving triumphantly in all his goings; "His banner over me is love!" A garland of victory awaits the victor's brow; "henceforth there is laid up for me a crown." And as for his spirits, they are festive in the love of the Lord, and they dance in the joy of blessed assurance. "I know in whom I have believed!" "I can do all things through Christ who strengtheneth me!" We are more than conquerors in the conquering fellowship of our holy and gracious Lord. And this song of the conqueror is intended to be sung by thee and me. O, let us believe it!

"Shall this divinely-urgéd heart
Half toward its glory move?
What! shall I love in part—in part
Yield to the Lord of love?
O sweetest freedom, Lord, to be
Thy love's full prisoner!
Take me all captive; make of me
A more than conqueror!"

Made in the USA
Monee, IL
13 February 2025

12179777R00046